The Unquiet Western Front
Britain's Role in Literature and History

Britain's outstanding military achievement in the First World War has been eclipsed by literary myths. Why has the Army's role on the Western Front been so seriously misrepresented? This book shows how myths have become deeply rooted, particularly in the inter-war period, in the 1960s when the war was rediscovered, and in the 1990s.

The outstanding 'anti-war' influences have been 'war poets', subalterns' trench memoirs, the book and film of *All Quiet on the Western Front*, and the play *Journey's End*. For a new generation in the 1960s the play and film of *Oh What a Lovely War* had a dramatic effect, while more recently *Blackadder* has been dominant. Until recently historians had either reinforced the myths, or had failed to counter them. Now, thanks to the opening of the official archives and a more objective approach by a new generation, the myths are being challenged. This book follows the intense controversy from 1918 to the present, and concludes that historians are at last permitting the First World War to be placed in proper perspective.

BRIAN BOND is Emeritus Professor of Military History, King's College London.

The Unquiet Western Front
Britain's Role in Literature and History

Brian Bond

CAMBRIDGE UNIVERSITY PRESS
Cambridge, New York, Melbourne, Madrid, Cape Town, Singapore, São Paulo

Cambridge University Press
The Edinburgh Building, Cambridge CB2 8RU, UK

Published in the United States of America by Cambridge University Press, New York

www.cambridge.org
Information on this title: www.cambridge.org/9780521809955

First published 2002
Reprinted 2004
This digitally printed version 2007

A catalogue record for this publication is available from the British Library

ISBN 978-0-521-80995-5 hardback
ISBN 978-0-521-03641-2 paperback

Contents

PREFACE AND ACKNOWLEDGEMENTS vii

1 THE NECESSARY WAR, 1914–1918 1

2 GOODBYE TO ALL THAT, 1919–1933 27

3 DONKEYS AND FLANDERS MUD
THE WAR REDISCOVERED IN THE 1960S 51

4 THINKING THE UNTHINKABLE
THE FIRST WORLD WAR AS HISTORY 75

SIR LEES KNOWLES (1857–1928) 102

THE LEES KNOWLES LECTURES 105

NOTES 109

SELECT BIBLIOGRAPHY 122

INDEX 125

Preface and acknowledgements

In delivering the annual Liddell Hart lecture at King's
College London in November 1997 I had an early opportunity to outline my views on the many myths and misrepresentations which have distorted British understanding of the nation's achievement in the First World War and,
more particularly, of the Army's role on the Western Front.
When, shortly afterwards, I was invited by Trinity College
Cambridge to give the prestigious Lees Knowles lectures in
2000 this seemed an ideal opportunity to examine this huge
and controversial subject in more detail and over a longer
period. The programme of four lectures, given under the
umbrella title 'Britain and the First World War: the challenge to historians', permitted me to pay more attention
to the 1960s, when earlier 'disenchanted' and profoundly
critical views of the First World War were rediscovered and
much developed. Part of my argument throughout has been
that military historians have in general failed to present a
positive interpretation of Britain's role in the war or, at
any rate, that their versions have been overwhelmed and
obliterated by the enormous impact of supposedly 'anti-war'

poetry, memoirs, novels, plays and films. While the best of these imaginative literary and personal interpretations have deservedly remained popular and influential they ignored, or failed to answer convincingly, the larger historical questions about political and strategic issues: what was the war 'about'? how was it fought? and why did Britain and her allies eventually emerge victorious? Fortunately, due in part to the availability of a much wider range of sources, but even more to changing perspectives and greater objectivity, really excellent military history began to be published in the last decade or so of the twentieth century. In my final lecture I therefore suggest that historians are now successfully challenging the deeply rooted notions of British 'butchers and bunglers', of 'lions led by donkeys', and of general disenchantment with an unnecessary, pointless and ultimately futile war.

In 1999 I was elected a Visiting Fellow of All Souls College, Oxford for the Hilary and Trinity terms 2000 and spent this idyllic interlude in preparing the four Lees Knowles lectures. I am most grateful to the Warden and Fellows for the many stimulating discussions of my research in progress, and especially for the opportunity to outline my ideas at the Visiting Fellows' seminar chaired by Robert O'Neill. I also presented a draft version of the second lecture at my former college, Worcester, where John Stevenson, James Campbell and other scholars offered some challenging comments.

My two short visits to Trinity College, Cambridge in November 2000 were somewhat overshadowed by anxiety about being flooded at home, as actually occurred a month later, but the kindness of the Master and Fellows still made this a most enjoyable and memorable occasion. I am especially indebted to Boyd Hilton for the great care he took in arranging and advertising the lectures, and for the splendid accommodation and festivities he laid on in college. Robert

Neild, Dennis Green and other Fellows went to great trouble to make my wife and me, and my guest Tony Hampshire, feel welcome. William Davies and representatives of Cambridge University Press offered early encouragement that my lectures would be published, and Philippa Youngman's exemplary copy-editing has saved me from numerous slips and obscurities.

In a concise survey of a vast topic such as this one inevitably incurs numerous debts to friends, colleagues and constructive critics which can only be briefly and inadequately acknowledged here. Correlli Barnett kindly suggested my name as a possible Lees Knowles lecturer and overcame difficulties to attend the series. Keith Jeffery, the previous lecturer whose outstanding book was published during my stay at Trinity College, gave me helpful advance information about the venue, likely numbers attending and arrangements in College. Stephen and Phylomena Badsey, Nigel and Terry Cave, and Gary Sheffield all read the lectures in draft after their delivery and pointed out numerous stylistic blemishes, factual errors and possible modifications and changes. I have adopted nearly all their suggestions but am, of course, entirely responsible for the final text. Alex Danchev also read and approved the third lecture in which I draw heavily on his contribution to a volume I had edited a decade earlier.

In addition to vetting the lectures in draft, Stephen Badsey, Gary Sheffield and Nigel Cave made available to me copies of articles, reviews, cassettes and other material as did Ian Beckett, Keith Grieves, Robin Brodhurst and Nicholas Hiley. They, and other helpers mentioned in the references, will recognise my indebtedness to them while, I hope, excusing me for not pursuing every topic to the extent or in the detail they might reasonably have expected.

I am grateful to the Liddell Hart Trustees for permission to quote from files in the Liddell Hart Centre for

Military Archives at King's College London. I have carefully checked the number and wordage of quotations from published works and believe that they fall within the permissible limits for scholarly discussion such as I have experienced with other historians' quotations from my own publications. However, should any author feel I have infringed his or her copyright I offer my sincere apologies.

It remains to acknowledge what is by far my greatest debt, to my wife Madeleine, for typing and retyping my longhand draft and suggesting numerous clarifications and stylistic improvements. Although this is a short book, it has been prepared for publication in particularly difficult circumstances due to the severe flooding of our home and the six months of chaotic disruption that resulted.

1 The necessary war, 1914–1918

The First World War continues to cast its long shadow over British culture and 'modern memory' at the beginning of the twenty-first century, and remains more controversial than the Second. Myths prevail over historical reality and today the earlier conflict is assumed to constitute 'the prime example of war as horror and futility'.[1] Yet, without claiming for it the accolade of 'a good war', as A. J. P. Taylor rather surprisingly did for the struggle against Nazi Germany, it was, for Britain, a necessary and successful war, and an outstanding achievement for a democratic nation in arms.

The following, I shall argue, are the main features in a positive interpretation of the British war effort. The Liberal government did not stumble heedlessly into war in 1914 but made a deliberate decision to prevent German domination of Europe. The tiny regular army of 1914 was transformed, with remarkable success, first into a predominantly citizens' volunteer body and then into the mass conscript force of 1917–18. The learning process was unavoidably painful and costly, but the British Army's performance compared well with that of both allies and opponents. In such a hectic expansion there were bound to be some 'duds' in higher command and staff appointments, but it would be difficult to name many 'butchers and bunglers' in the latter part of the war: popular notions about this are based on ignorance. Military morale, although brittle at times, held firm through all the setbacks and heavy casualties. Popular support also remained steady, although changing from early euphoria to a dogged determination to see it through. Contrary to popular belief, official propaganda played an insignificant part in sustaining morale on the home front. British and dominion forces played the leading role in the final victorious advance in 1918 on the all-important Western Front. In the post-war settlement Britain achieved most of its objectives with regard to Europe, and its empire expanded to its greatest extent. It was not the fault of those who won the war on the battlefields that the anticipated rewards soon appeared to be disappointing. Indeed on the international stage it was largely beyond Britain's control that the terms of the Treaty of Versailles could not be enforced, and that Germany again became a threat within fifteen years.

It is once again fashionable to query the necessity for Britain's decision to enter the First World War. Counterfactual speculation presents a seductive vision of a neutral Britain avoiding casualties and financial decline, and living in economic harmony with a victorious Germany. Moreover, we are asked to believe, a different decision by Britain in August 1914 would have prevented the Russian Revolution, the communist and Nazi regimes and most of the evils of the twentieth century. This is heady stuff but it is not a meaningful enterprise for historians.

While it was far from certain – let alone inevitable – in the summer of 1914 that Britain and Germany would soon be at war, intense rivalry and antagonism had been building up between them for several decades. As Paul Kennedy

has shown,[2] Britain was alarmed by Germany's rapid industrial and population growth; it was vastly superior to
France according to virtually every criterion, notably in
military power; and Russia's ability to offset this disparity
was 'blown to the winds' by defeat and revolution in 1905.
Even more disturbing, Germany's rapid naval expansion
posed a clear challenge to Britain's security to which the
latter was bound to respond. As Kennedy comments, it is
not necessary for the historian to judge whether Britain
or Germany was right or wrong in this 'struggle for mas-
tery', but the latter's aggressive rhetoric and sabre-rattling
underlined the (correct) impression that it was prepared to
resort to war to challenge the status quo. It was essentially a
matter of timing a pre-emptive strike. Consequently, when
every allowance is made for Germany's domestic and al-
liance problems in 1914, the fact remains that 'virtually all
the tangled wires of causality led back to Berlin'. In particular, it was the 'sublime genius of the Prussian General
Staff', by its reckless concentration on a western offensive whatever the immediate cause of hostilities – namely
Austria-Hungary's determination to make war on Serbia –
which brought the (by then latent) Anglo-German antagonism to the brink of war.[3]

On the British side insurance against the perceived
German threat was manifested in a treaty with Japan (1902)
and ententes with France (1904) and Russia (1907). These
arrangements have been widely regarded by historians as
a diplomatic triumph.[4] In themselves they did not commit
Britain to a war on the Continent, nor did the military and
naval conversations with France that ensued. Nevertheless
they did make it extremely doubtful that Britain could remain neutral in the event of a general war resulting from a
German offensive against France.

Michael Brock has shown that as the July 1914 crisis in-
tensified, the Prime Minister, Herbert Asquith, his leading
Cabinet colleagues and military advisers remained confident

that a limited German advance through southern Belgium would not oblige Britain to declare war.[5] The King was informed as late as 29 July that Britain's involvement was unlikely. Yet by 2 August the government was swinging towards intervention. This was due to the fact that France seemed in danger of defeat, and Sir Edward Grey, the Foreign Secretary, in particular, was under pressure from popular opinion and the Foreign Office to offer British support, though perhaps short of full intervention.

What resolved the government's doubts and ended its hesitation was Germany's brutal ultimatum demanding unimpeded passage through the whole of Belgium followed by the news, on 3 August, of the latter's refusal and of King Albert's appeal to King George V for diplomatic support. On the next day the German invasion began and Britain promptly entered the war. It would not be unduly cynical to comment that, while there was fervent support for the rescue of 'poor little Belgium', Britain's intervention was motivated primarily by self-interest: a sudden realization of the strategic dangers that a rapid German conquest of France and Belgium would entail.[6]

Party political considerations played a crucial role in shaping the government's actions. Already, on 2 August, before the German ultimatum to Belgium, the Conservatives had pledged their support to Asquith in support of France. This strengthened Grey's hand and undermined the hopes of waverers that a pacifist stand could be effective. Several Cabinet members confided to friends that it was better to go to war united than to endure a coalition or even risk a complete withdrawal from office. Ministers also deluded themselves that they could wage war and control domestic politics by *liberal* methods.

One prominent minister in particular embodied these dilemmas. Lloyd George abandoned his pacifist stance and supported the declaration of war, ostensibly because of

Belgium, but really because he believed that Britain's fate was linked to that of France and it would be a political disaster to allow the Cabinet to be split over such a vital issue.[7] In these circumstances it seems virtually impossible to believe that Britain could have remained neutral. The only issues were whether Britain would intervene at once or later, and with a divided or united government and popular support. In the event Asquith had achieved a remarkable, albeit short-lived, triumph: a Liberal government had embarked upon a continental war with only minor defections from the Cabinet, with strong party, opposition and parliamentary backing, and with bellicose popular support that outstripped that of the decision-makers in its fervour.

It is one of the paradoxes of this culmination of the Anglo-German antagonism that neither had been seriously considering war against the other when the crisis began: Britain because it was preoccupied with the real possibility of civil war in Ireland, and Germany because its faith in a short-war victory made the involvement of the tiny British Expeditionary Force (BEF) and Britain's formidable navy seem irrelevant.

However, while it is true that Germany had no immediate war aims against Britain, it is clear that an early victory over France would have had disastrous consequences. Bethmann Hollweg's September Programme, drawn up in anticipation of imminent peace negotiations with a defeated France, spoke of so weakening the latter that its revival as a great power would be impossible for all time. The military leaders were to decide on various possible annexations, including the coastal strip from Dunkirk to Boulogne. A commercial treaty would render France dependent on Germany and permit the exclusion of British commerce from France. Belgium would be, at the very least, reduced to a vassal state dependent on Germany with the possibility of incorporating French Flanders. The 'competent quarters' (that is, the

German General Staff) would have to judge the military value against Britain of these arrangements. Most important of all, victory would usher in a central European economic association dominated by Germany and with Britain pointedly excluded from the list of members.[8]

Thus Britain's decision to enter the war, although forced on it by an unexpected chain of events, may be viewed as both calculated and also justified by fears of what penalties might result from neutrality. Britain (and the dominions) fought the war first and foremost to preserve its independence and status as a great imperial power by resisting the domination of Europe by the Central Powers. But a second purpose, less evident until the late stages of the war, was to gain a peace settlement which would also enhance Britain's and its Empire's security vis-à-vis its allies and co-belligerents – France, Russia and, to a lesser extent, the United States.[9]

There was, however, a serious flaw in the government's assumptions about a war whose duration and nature it completely failed to comprehend. The government, in effect, hoped to wage a short war in terms of blockading Germany, supplying its allies with money and munitions, and despatching the modest BEF to France essentially as a token of good intent. In view of accurate pre-war assessments of Germany's industrial and military power, this stance in 1914 was highly unrealistic and was soon to be exposed as such.[10]

With the wisdom of hindsight it is tempting to argue that there must have been a better alternative to the bloodletting and destruction between 1914 and 1918. While this notion can be debated endlessly as regards the general causes of the First World War, it has little bearing on the specific issue of Anglo-German antagonism. As Paul Kennedy concludes, by making minor concessions Britain 'might have papered over the cracks in the Anglo-German relationship for a few more years, but it is difficult to see how such gestures would have altered the elemental German push to change the existing distribution of power', which was always likely to provoke a strong British reaction. Unless one of the rivals was prepared to introduce a drastic change of policy their vital interests would remain diametrically opposed. Essentially, in 1914 Britain was prepared to fight to preserve the existing status quo whereas Germany, for a mixture of offensive and defensive motives, was determined to alter it.[11]

Finally, in summing up the reasons for Britain entering the war, it is important to consider the mental outlook or moral code of thoughtful people in the very different ethos of 1914. Ignorance of the sordid realities of war allowed free play to the notion of a liberal crusade against uncivilized behaviour. If a great power were allowed to break an international agreement and invade a small neighbour with impunity, then European civilization would be seriously undermined. This outlook seemed to be accepted by all social classes and persisted to a remarkable extent for much of the war, even after the appalling costs had become clear.[12]

It cannot be over-emphasized that, when declaring war in August 1914 and despatching the small BEF to France, the government had no intention of fighting a long and costly 'total war'. Conscription, in particular, was anathema to most Liberals. Even Lord Kitchener, the imperial proconsul appointed as War Minister to inspire confidence, who *did* envisage a long war from the outset, could not foresee the pressures which the Central Powers' early successes in both east and west would impose on the Entente.

Kitchener's plan was that his volunteer New Armies, raised in 1914–15, should be conserved as much as possible to ensure that Britain would be the strongest military power at the peace conference. The French and Russian armies would bear the brunt of attrition warfare in 1915–16 before the British forces intervened in strength to deal the decisive blow. This calculated strategy was undermined by enormous French losses in the first year of the war, by similar Russian losses and a hectic retreat in the summer of 1915, and by Britain's failure at the Dardanelles. Consequently, in mid-1915, British policy-makers were reluctantly forced to conclude that, in order to save the Entente, its forces must play a full part in the continental land war. The disastrous battle of Loos in September 1915 marked the first stage in this drastic change of policy, the adoption of conscription early in 1916 the second stage, and the Somme campaign the third. The proponents of a limited war effort using only volunteer forces were overwhelmed by events. The risk of heavy casualties and bankruptcy seemed preferable to defeat.[13]

In retrospect it is tempting to believe that either group of allies would have done better to negotiate a 'peace without victory' once the initial hopes of a quick decision had been thwarted. But the trajectory of the war and the myriad conflicting interests involved suggest that this was never a realistic option. Germany's extensive territorial gains in 1914 and 1915 did not incline its leaders to moderation, and even the severe effects of attrition at Verdun and on the Somme in 1916 were offset by victory over Romania and confidence that Russia was tottering towards defeat. Indeed the Central Powers' Peace Note in December 1916 was prompted largely by the victory in Romania; its tone was bellicose and no specific conditions were mentioned. The Entente correctly assumed that the terms would be unacceptable. Bethmann's annexation proposals were in fact made harsher on every point by Hindenburg and Ludendorff: they opposed any territorial cession to France, required Luxembourg to be annexed, and demanded that the Belgian and Polish economies be subordinated to Germany's. After the Entente's rejection of the Note,

Hindenburg hardened his position further, demanding additional annexations in east and west. The military, naval and colonial authorities all grew more extreme in their demands. In short, German high-level decision-making was a shambles, with the military leaders increasingly dominant and unwilling to compromise.[14]

On the British side, the conflict was presented as not only a traditional strategy to defend the home islands and the empire, but also as a crusade for a more peaceful and democratic world order. As David Stevenson has pointed out, British policy 'combined uncertainty and even altruism within Europe with *Realpolitik* outside'. Above all, Germany must be destroyed as a colonial and naval threat. Britain had no territorial claims against Germany, but the rhetorical aim of 'smashing Prussian militarism' could only be achieved, if indeed at all, through a decisive military victory. Though flexible in some respects about a settlement with Germany, Lloyd George was committed to 'punishing aggression' and 'promoting democratisation'. Consequently Britain 'remained far removed from a negotiated settlement with the Central Powers'. Even the defection of Russia and the intervention of the United States in 1917 did not alter the fundamental conviction that only a clear-cut victory would make possible a lasting peace. The extremely harsh terms which Germany imposed on Russia in the Treaty of Brest-Litovsk (March 1918), followed by a drive deep into the Caucasus, beyond the treaty's terms, demonstrated what penalties the Western Powers might expect if they were defeated. President Woodrow Wilson was also now convinced that a just and lasting peace could only follow after the clear military defeat of the Central Powers.[15]

It is very difficult now, particularly in comparison with the Second World War, to interpret the First World War in ideological terms. Yet without a powerful input of idealism it is impossible to understand why Liberal intellectuals such as C. E. Montague were so enthusiastic at the outbreak of war, and why 'liberal opinion' continued to support the war when its appalling costs became clear. The notion of the conflict as a crusade on behalf of liberal idealism embodied a startling paradox: war would be waged to remove the causes of war.[16] An Entente victory, despite the embarrassment of tsarist Russia as an ally, would entail the defeat of 'militarism'. These lofty ideals sat uneasily with more tangible political goals such as the restoration of Belgian independence and the defeat of the German navy.

From the very outset German actions were, to say the least, careless and reckless with regard to neutral opinion and enemy propaganda. The flagrant violation of Belgian neutrality made Germany an international pariah. The destruction of the mediaeval library at Louvain and the Cloth Hall at Ypres, the murder of Belgian civilians and the first large-scale use of poison gas in 1915 all outraged civilized opinion. Even where the line between humanitarian restraint and military necessity was blurred – as in the sinking of the passenger liner *Lusitania* – a German firm presented a propaganda gift to their opponents by striking a vainglorious commemorative medal. British morale was continuously fuelled by moral outrage at enemy atrocities. Consequently, in John Bourne's striking summary, 'British public opinion camped throughout the war on the moral high ground, [and] Asquith pitched the first tent' with his rhetoric of fighting for principles 'vital to the civilisation of the world'.[17]

Although 'propaganda', in the sense of exploiting news to the full, sometimes without undue concern for strict accuracy, was employed by all sides and to an extent that may strike us now as disgraceful and nauseating, its importance as regards home morale must not be exaggerated. Propaganda could sustain morale by blackening the enemy's image and gilding one's own, but it could not create high morale in the face of harsh realities such as poor working conditions and obvious military failures.

Indeed, contrary to earlier assumptions, we now have ample evidence that official efforts to mould public opinion, for example through censorship and propaganda of various kinds, were of marginal importance. Censorship of the press was inconsistent and astonishingly lax, but this hardly mattered given the press barons' conviction that newspapers had a duty to maintain civilian morale and support the army. This meant in practice that the mass circulation dailies did all they could to stress the justice of Britain's cause and, equally important, to deny a platform to individuals or groups who did not. Consequently, the press was consistently hostile to pacifists, conscientious objectors, strikers and any group deemed to be hindering the war effort. As a corollary, important sections of the press believed that it was the duty of politicians to give all possible support to the army and then stand back and allow the generals to win the war. This useful conduit was cleverly exploited by general headquarters (GHQ) in France, not always with scrupulous accuracy. Optimistic news from the front brought short-term benefits to morale at home but resulted later in a backlash against the concealment of painful truths and, worse, outright deception.

Beyond these considerations, we have to remember that in the pre-television age, the public's grasp of the nature of war was very defective. In fact 'a curtain of unreality descended between the war and the public perceptions of it'. Even the more popular newspapers made few concessions with their lofty style to the interests of mass culture, and war reporters were severely handicapped by military censorship and by the practical difficulties of witnessing front-line action. Unlike the French, the British had no official photographers or cameramen at the front until early 1916. Eventually there were sixteen photographers for all the war

theatres. Furthermore, most reporters were severely con-
strained by their own patriotic conception of their role, and
by lack of an adequate style and vocabulary to convey the
harsh realities of combat.[18] Here, we may suggest, modern
critics such as Paul Fussell have a legitimate target in the
gulf, which we now perceive as shocking, between 'the real
war' and the sanitized, anodyne version presented to the
public.

We must, however, avoid the trap of believing that two
conflicting views of the war existed in British society between 1914 and 1918: the 'true view', stressing waste and
horror, belonging to the fighting soldiers, and the 'false
view', that of deluded civilian belief in patriotism and
the nobility of sacrifice.[19] A corollary of this myth is that
the government established such a firm control over all the
news media that it was able to deceive the public into see-
ing the war in a false light. Nick Hiley has exploded these
myths. The Parliamentary Recruiting Committee, for example, at the outset launched a big poster campaign, but
this still represented less than 1 per cent of the commercial
poster advertising budget in the normal year. Moreover,
none of its posters were designed by government officials.
Contrary to popular belief, there is no evidence of any official involvement in the famous poster of Lord Kitchener
carrying the slogan 'Your Country Needs You'. This and
other posters represented a much larger set of patriotic images in general circulation. A similarly negative conclusion may be reached about official propaganda in the cinema. Although nearly 200 official films, including features,
shorts and cartoons, were produced in the latter half of
the war, this was still minuscule in comparison with commercial productions. At no time in the war, states Hiley,
were as many cameramen employed in official filming as
a single company would have used before 1914 to cover
the Grand National. The Press Bureau's ability to shape

public opinion has also been greatly exaggerated: it was a
small organization, totally reliant on newspaper support,
primarily concerned with a select group of Fleet Street papers thought to be politically influential. In fact, far from
tightening their grip on public opinion, official news media
were swamped by sources quite outside official control. In
any case, the Great War was largely conveyed to the public
in pre-1914 imagery and concepts: 'only during the 1920s
and 1930s was it re-fought using new images of waste and
destruction developed during the conflict. It is this later re-
evaluation that has come down to us as the true picture of
British society during the Great War, but it is an historical
absurdity'.[20]

Hiley's thesis is borne out by public reaction to the famous official film *The Battle of the Somme*, which drew
enormous audiences when first shown in August 1916, that
is, while the campaign was still in progress. Whereas contemporary viewers are apt to interpret the film as powerful evidence of the horror and futility of war, those at
the time, assuming the cause to be just, seem to have been
strengthened in their resolve to persevere to achieve victory. The film, by first showing dead British soldiers, as
well as Germans, positively helped to give viewers some
idea of what war was really like. Another official film, *The
Battle of the Ancre and the Advance of the Tanks*, was also
hugely popular, in part because it exploited the novelty of
Britain's new wonder-weapon, the tank, but also because
it vividly conveyed the dignity of ordinary soldiers doing
their duty in a desolate battlescape. However, the next official war film, *The German Retreat and the Battle of Arras*,
shown in June 1917, proved to be such a box-office failure
that no more feature-length battle films were made during
the war. The public's desertion of cinemas showing official
war films was partly due to the government's understandable reluctance to show more footage of British dead and

wounded soldiers in appalling battlefield conditions, hence their reversion to anodyne scenes of cheerful Tommies relaxing and enjoying meals at ease in the rear areas. The War Office did, however, continue to produce short films, often dealing with more exotic aspects of the war, such as the campaigns in Palestine and Mesopotamia. A wider explanation must include the effects of growing hardship on ordinary people, who showed some signs of bitterness against the privileged classes as the war dragged on interminably. However, the dramatic German breakthrough and advance in March 1918 once again raised fears of defeat and caused the nation to rally against the enemy.[21]

Although numerous *individuals* wrote bitterly about their war experience and some evidently suffered from low morale, military morale in war time is essentially about the attitudes, cohesion and combat effectiveness of *groups*, ranging from the platoon and company right up to divisions, corps and armies. Scholarly consensus is that the British Army's morale remained high (or, at worst, steady), with the vast majority of soldiers displaying 'fighting spirit'. This was an impressive achievement for an overwhelmingly non-professional force which endured tremendous hardships and heavy casualties but continued to fight effectively.

The picture was not of course uniformly rosy, and there are known cases of battalions fleeing in disorder or being routed without putting up a fight, particularly on the Somme in 1916 and during the March retreat in 1918.[22] On the evidence mainly of censored letters, morale reached its lowest point during the later stages of the Passchendaele campaign in 1917, but even then there was no collective indiscipline comparable to the French mutinies a few months earlier. Indeed, the only serious example of indiscipline amounting to rebellion or mutiny *during the war* occurred at the notorious base training camp at Etaples in September 1917.[23] Here conditions were highly unusual:

experienced troops were treated like raw recruits, officers were separated from their men so that protective paternalism was lacking, and outrage was directed mainly at military police and NCO instructors. Without the 'creative tension' that existed at unit level between rigorous discipline and paternalism based on common pride in the battalion there would surely have been mutinies in the combat zone. The regular army's harsh disciplinary code is now much criticized but it was less resented then, given the severity of punishments in civil life.[24] Heavy losses in battle could cause morale to plummet for a short time, but rest, good food and above all minor but significant victories could have a prompt restorative effect. The British citizen soldiers were notorious grumblers and 'moaners' whose mood could fluctuate sharply. But their performance was rarely less than dogged. In their determination to defeat the Germans their morale reflected that of the nation-in-arms as a whole. Strong emotions of hatred of the enemy and lust for revenge must also be taken into account. Military and civilian morale were probably as high in November 1918 as at any point during the war. 'Trench warfare was a terrible experience, but the prospects of defeat at the hands of Germany were worse.'[25]

One famous subaltern and war poet who *did* briefly renounce the pull of comradeship, loyalty to his men and regimental tradition to stage a personal rebellion was Siegfried Sassoon. It is important to discuss this episode here because it contributed significantly to the post-war image of the war poets and their supposed anti-war stance.

Sassoon was a brave, competent and, at times, ferocious warrior serving with the Royal Welch Fusiliers. In June 1917 he invited a court martial and disgrace by denouncing the war as unjust in a statement to a Member of Parliament which then appeared in the press. In addition he resigned his commission and threw the ribbons of his Military Cross into the river Mersey. The anti-climactic outcome of this courageous but foolhardy gesture is very well known thanks to recent coverage in a bestselling novel and the subsequent film.[26] Through the intervention of his friend and fellow-officer in the Royal Welch Fusiliers, Robert Graves, Sassoon was treated as a shell-shock case and became a patient in Craiglockhart Hospital near Edinburgh whence he later returned to duty at the front. Sassoon's own autobiographical writing reveals his confused state of mind and this is amplified in a recent biography.[27]

When Sassoon's endurance snapped his chief target was the ignorance and complacency of pro-war civilians. In diaries and letters he raged against profiteers, shirkers, clerics and especially women – including even war widows. He realized at the time that much of his bile was due to an unhealthy lifestyle in England: he would, he believed, be fitter and better in spirits once back with his battalion. Before that, however, he fell under the spell of Lady Ottoline Morrell and her Garsington circle. He was strongly influenced in particular by Bertrand Russell and H. G. Wells, who persuaded him that the British government had spurned genuine German peace offers and was now waging a war of aggression. Although in his published statement Sassoon explicitly excluded the military conduct of the war from his protest, he was in fact very angry and depressed by the heavy losses his battalion had recently suffered, and feared that the war would eventually be lost after several more years of pointless bloodshed. The essence of his protest was as follows:

> I believe that this War, upon which I entered as a war
> of defence and liberation, has now become a war of
> aggression and conquest. I believe that the purposes for
> which I and my fellow soldiers entered upon this War
> should have been so clearly stated as to have made it

> impossible for them to be changed without our knowledge,
> and that, had this been done, the objects which actuated
> us would now have been attainable by negotiation.
>
> I have seen and endured the sufferings of the troops,
> and I can no longer be a party to prolonging those
> sufferings for ends which I believe to be evil and unjust.[28]

Sassoon was a good officer and, at his best, an impressive poet, but in his rage and bitterness, due partly to personal hang-ups and partly to a natural reaction to conditions at the front and their misrepresentation at home, he lashed out blindly. Thus he composed a savage poem about General Rawlinson, calling him 'the corpse commander', and, with unintended irony, was inspired to write 'The General' by a glimpse of Sir Ivor Maxe, one of the best commanders on the Western Front.

But of course the main criticism to be made against his protest was that it was politically unacceptable and impractical. This he later acknowledged while not regretting his action:

> I must add that in the light of the subsequent events it is
> difficult to believe that a Peace negotiated in 1917 would
> have been permanent. I share the general opinion that
> nothing on earth would have prevented a recurrence of
> Teutonic aggressiveness.[29]

No one can study the First World War, even superficially, without realizing that senior commanders and staff officers made numerous mistakes, particularly in renewing and prolonging offensives which had bogged down, thus contributing to the heavy loss of life – the main charge against them ever since. Even after ammunition and equipment became more plentiful, by mid-1916, and a learning process was clearly in being, operational progress was still patchy and earlier errors might be repeated.[30] Nevertheless, military historians deeply resent the tendency to dwell obsessively on the most obvious examples of failure – notably the first day of the Somme campaign in 1916 and the later stages of the Third Ypres offensive in 1917 – while showing little interest in, or appreciation of, the nation's unique and ultimately successful war effort over the whole period 1914–18. Changes in press policy also contributed to the neglect of the British Army's achievements in 1918. Haig's former supporters, Beaverbrook, Rothermere and Northcliffe, were now in, or associated with, the government and tended to adopt the Whitehall perspective. For their parts, Haig and general headquarters (GHQ) did little to win back press support. In consequence 'there was no policy or desire either in Whitehall or at GHQ ... to publicise the British victories of later in the year'.[31]

A brief reference to the unexpected, rapid and enormous expansion of the army will help to explain why it took so long for Britain to compete effectively in full-scale continental warfare. The professional, and mostly-regular, BEF of 1914 consisted of only six lightly equipped divisions: by 1918 there were more than sixty British divisions on the Western Front alone, by now composed mainly of conscripts and numbering about two million men. The Royal Artillery became the dominant arm on the battlefield – an 'army within the army' of half a million gunners, that is, twice the size of the whole BEF in 1914. Few British generals had had any experience of high command (that is: a division or a corps) before 1914, and even for these few, conditions on the Western Front soon proved to be very different from the South African veldt. The Staff College at Camberley had produced only a few hundred trained staff officers – too few even to meet the initial needs of the War Office, the training depots and the BEF – let alone the vast expansion immediately signalled by the recruitment of the volunteer new armies in 1914–15. Not surprisingly this largely improvised citizen army showed many deficiencies in the first two years of the war, notably at Loos, and was then prematurely obliged to take on the major offensive role from mid-1916 onwards.[32]

Contrary to popular myth the army was generally well led. Indeed, Sir John Keegan has suggested that British military leadership – 'conscious, principled, exemplary' – was of higher quality and significance in the First World War than before or since. Regimental officers lived close to their men and shared their privations and dangers to a considerable degree. Proportionately, junior officers suffered significantly higher casualties than the other ranks. The officer corps also changed in social composition in step with the vast expansion in the ranks. There were a substantial number of working-class and lower middle-class officers, so that ex-public schoolboys did not retain their early dominance, if only because so many were killed. In the middle and higher commands few 'duds' or incompetents survived; indeed many sound but insufficiently aggressive divisional and brigade commanders were sacked in the ruthless drive for efficiency. British staff officers in the First World War have had a bad press, from war poets speaking for disgruntled rankers and from later critics largely ignorant of the subject. We need only note here that in the operational staff of GHQ and higher formations many officers – such as Bernard Montgomery and John Dill – were former and future combat commanders, and that many were killed or wounded. They were comparatively few in number (only six to a division) and worked long hours under tremendous pressure. As for the 'Q' or administrative staff, it is fair to say that they did an excellent job in feeding, supplying, training and providing medical care for this vast army. In sum, this amateur force of citizens in uniform learned how to conduct modern industrial warfare in quite unexpected siege conditions against what was surely the world's toughest and most tactically adept enemy, the imperial German army.[33]

Britain's unprecedented national war effort was widely appreciated in the hour of victory, as we should expect, since nearly every family in the land had contributed to it, but it was later to be downplayed and even forgotten as the disappointing results of the conflict were applied retrospectively to the war itself. In recent decades (as I shall discuss more fully in the final chapter) military historians have stressed the positive achievements of the 'nation in arms'[34] and, in the operational sphere, broadly accept the notion of a 'learning curve'. Indeed, with the odd exception such as Sir John Keegan, who rejects this endeavour,[35] the debate has moved on to specific issues, such as the origins of the process, the rapidity or 'steepness' of the curve, the levels at which lessons were implemented and who deserves the credit.

Unfortunately many critics who do not accept these interpretations are still metaphorically bogged down in the attrition battles of 1916 and 1917, and find it hard to come to terms with the culminating victorious advance of 1918 when British and imperial forces played the leading role in defeating the German armies on the Western Front. As I remarked in my Liddell Hart Lecture in 1997:

> Between 18 July and 11 November the British forces took 188, 700 prisoners and 2,840 guns, far more in each category than the French, Americans and Belgians. Following the brilliant operations in late September to break through the Hindenburg Line, the five British armies skilfully outmanouevred the stubborn defenders from a series of river and canal lines on which Ludendorff had hoped to stabilise the front during the winter.
>
> Conditions did not permit a breakthrough and the advance to victory was steady rather than dramatic – about

sixty miles at an average rate of less than a mile per day.
The Germans fought stubbornly against superior artillery
assisted by dominant allied air forces. Despite a few cases
of large-scale surrenders there was no general
disintegration. Nevertheless the imminence of complete
defeat was demonstrated by Ludendorff's resignation and
the acceptance of armistice terms which precluded any
hope of renewing the struggle.[36]

The key tactical development between 1916 and 1918
was the provision of accurate artillery protection for advancing infantry. By employing a combination of heavy
guns, mortars, machineguns, tanks and aircraft, the British
could dominate the enemy's artillery and trench defences
and get their infantry forward in short advances under
this fire cover.[37] This was made evident at Cambrai in
November 1917, and was demonstrated on a large scale
on the first day of the battle of Amiens (8 August 1918) and
continued on successive days. The most impressive success for these 'bite and hold' tactics was the breaking of
the formidable Hindenburg line at the end of September.
Although military historians are still debating the relative
contributions of different weapons and weapons systems –
artillery, tanks, aircraft – to the final victory, the outstanding
development lay in the better co-ordination of the various
elements:

> As a result of meticulous planning, each component was
> integrated with, and provided maximum support for,
> every other component. Here, more than anywhere else,
> was the great technical achievement of these climactic
> battles. It was not that the British had developed a
> war-winning weapon. What they had produced was a
> weapons system: the melding of the various elements in
> the military arm into a mutually supporting whole.[38]

There had clearly been a transformation, if not indeed a revolution, in the style of conducting war between 1914 and 1918: from recognizably nineteenth-century weapons and tactics at the outset, the BEF at the end of the war was practising the essential components of the modern all-arms battle. Consequently, Gary Sheffield does not seem to me to be overstating the case in writing that

> In terms of the size and power of the enemy army that was defeated and the high degree of military skill that was demonstrated, 1918 is the greatest victory in British military history.[39]

At the end of the First World War and for several years afterwards the importance of victory was well understood. As Hugh Dalton would later remark, 'No difference between victors and vanquished? A foolish fable. The Germans didn't believe it after 1918. We shouldn't have believed if they had won. We shan't believe [it] if they win next time'.[40]

Despite his grave doubts about Haig's strategy, Lloyd George and other ministers continued to believe during the war that Britain's human, economic and financial costs and sacrifices were necessary. Britain and France, which had made the greatest contribution to victory, emerged as the main beneficiaries. Britain, in particular, achieved most of its practical war aims: the German navy was destroyed and its army's capabilities drastically restricted; French and Belgian independence was restored and the former regained Alsace and Lorraine. Germany's drive to dominate Europe had been checked for the foreseeable future.[41] Britain had also secured most of its imperial aims both in holding off French and Russian rivalry in the Near and Middle East, and in acquiring 'mandates' in the former Ottoman Empire which extended its own empire to its greatest geographical extent.

Nor should the fruits of victory be envisaged in purely territorial or security terms. What of the wartime idealism which believed the conflict to be one between the liberal democracy of the Western Allies and the predatory military autocracy of the Central Powers? As Trevor Wilson boldly put it, if the First World War could hardly be described as 'a good war', was it not nevertheless 'one of freedom's battles?'[42] But, as he also notes, there was bound to be disappointment on the part of idealists who had taken grandiose wartime promises too seriously: Britain and its continental allies lacked both the power and political commitment to 'overthrow German militarism', whilst the notion that this was a 'war to end all wars' betrayed a sublime ignorance of the harsh realities of international relations. Nonetheless, Britain's willingness to sacrifice more than a million men to defend her interests on the Continent had deeply impressed her enemies.[43] Not for the first or the last time Britain's armed forces had gained immense prestige by their fighting prowess. This intangible advantage should be even more apparent now, when even the most powerful country on earth is reluctant to risk losing any of its citizens' lives in combat. Unfortunately Britain's political leaders in the 1930s seemed either unaware of this diplomatic asset or too preoccupied with the human and economic costs of the war to use it. This was most depressingly obvious during the Munich crisis. Thus was defeatism plucked from the garland of victory.

The notion of a rapid transition from public euphoria in 1918 to disenchantment by the mid-1920s is a complex phenomenon which I shall discuss further in the next chapter. But we need not look far to grasp the main reasons why rejoicing at the successful conclusion of a terrible war was so transient. Post-1918 Britain was far from resembling 'a land fit for heroes'. As the war was ending the Spanish influenza epidemic dealt a terrible blow to the public's morale. There were serious problems over demobilization – which caused more overt acts of military indiscipline than at any time during the war. The country was soon burdened with high unemployment, widespread and bitter strikes which seemed to threaten revolution, and civil war in Ireland. Second, the armistice and peace treaties with the Central Powers by no means signalled a clear and definite end to the First World War: civil war raged throughout the former tsarist empire; German *Freikorps* continued fighting in the Baltic states; and Turkey fought Greece in the Aegean, at one stage coming close to involving the British in another war at the Dardanelles. Third, the belated impact of casualty figures profoundly affected the whole nation. Surprisingly, the huge scale of the casualties seems to have made little impact on morale during the war. This was only in small part due to censorship: in fact casualty lists were regularly published by the leading national newspapers until the later stages of the war, and the provincial press continued to print the names of all victims, often accompanied by photographs. Despite this grim evidence a spirit of stoic endurance persisted. The idea of sacrifice in a just cause did not collapse into cynicism for the war generation. But this was not true of the generation which followed for whom 'The war lit a slow fuse under the values which had done most to sustain it'.[44]

As the most careful recent analysis by Jay Winter has suggested, the deaths directly related to combat of 722,785 British soldiers was not demographically significant.[45] Except as regards the quality and potential of upper- and middle-class officers who suffered disproportionate casualties, the notion of a 'lost generation' was exaggerated. But the social and cultural effects *were* profound and enduring. For example, more than half a million of those who died were aged under 30, and about 90 per cent of the fatalities came from the working class.

Thus there began, soon after the Armistice, two decades of national mourning behind a facade of hectic gaiety whose monumental, social and religious aspects are now interesting scholars.[46] Scarcely had the guns stopped firing than tourists began to visit the gruesome makeshift cemeteries, gradually to be transformed into beautiful and deeply moving religious sites resembling English gardens. On 11 November 1920 the Unknown Warrior was carried from France and buried in Westminster Abbey. British shipments of headstones to France numbered about four thousand a week for several years.[47] Huge memorials were raised at Thiepval, Ypres (the Menin Gate) and elsewhere, containing the names of tens of thousands of soldiers with no known grave (some 73,400 names at Thiepval alone). At home memorials were commissioned for churches and public places in cities, towns and villages throughout the land. Only a handful of villages in the whole kingdom claimed the enviable distinction of having no fatalities.[48]

These memorials and monuments remind us that British fatalities in the armed forces between 1914 and 1918 were greater than those in the Second World War by a ratio of three or four to one. In these circumstances there was an understandable tendency to repress memories of the recent war. The possibility of fighting another great war against Germany within a generation could not be contemplated. For most people war had been stripped of its last vestiges of romance. If it had formerly been accepted as an 'instrument of policy' it was so no longer. With every passing year the costs of the recent war loomed larger while its benefits became harder to appreciate. It was natural to blame all the disappointments of the post-war world on to the war itself, whereas benefits such as the restoration and extension of a democratic system, greater freedom and opportunities for women, the avoidance of revolution, and the generally sound discipline of the armed forces were taken for

granted. Even more imponderable were the alternative developments (now termed 'counter-factuals') which might
have occurred had Britain not taken part in the war at all.

In fact the 'real', historical war abruptly ceased to exist
in November 1918. 'Thereafter it was swallowed by imagination in the guise of memory.'[49] Only a few historians
sought to preserve, order and interpret the events of the
war objectively, and in the short term theirs was not the
approach which the public needed.

The resurrection and reworking of the First World War
largely in terms of individual experience in the form of
novels, memoirs and 'war literature' in general will form
the subject of my second chapter.

2 Goodbye to all that, 1919–1933

Thirty years ago Correlli Barnett published a fierce critique of British 'anti-war' literature in the 1920s from a
historian's viewpoint. Although his overall thesis, namely
that the anti-war literature seriously undermined the public's readiness to resist Nazism in the 1930s, differs from
mine, nevertheless his indictment still provides a firm basis
for my own account.[1]

Barnett pointed out that most of the best-known memoirs
and novels were written by ex-public school temporary officers who were much more sensitive and imaginative than
the vast majority of their comrades. They reacted excessively to the privations and miseries inseparable from all
wars which the hardier, tougher other ranks endured phleg-
matically; indeed he suggested that in some respects they,
the ordinary soldiers, were better off than in 'civvy street'.
Like earlier critics such as Cyril Falls, Barnett accused the
'anti-war' writers of focusing obsessively on 'the horrors'
of combat thereby distorting the complex reality of military experience and, incidentally, masking the fact that
they were killers as well as victims. Most important of all,

because these writers were concerned with conveying personal experiences as vividly as possible, and anyway had a limited perspective, they largely evaded the crucial issues of what the war was 'about' – both on the political and strategic levels. This huge omission was understandable, since they were still close to disturbing events, and did not claim to be historians, but later commentators too often ignored these limitations.

In this chapter I intend to discuss definitions of what it meant to be an 'anti-war' writer circa 1929 and to suggest that the influence of this literature was more restricted than is generally assumed. I also wish to advance the paradox that the 'anti-war' writers have exerted more influence on public opinion since the 1960s than they did in the 1930s. To take just one example, Wilfred Owen's poetry was little known in 1930, whereas Rupert Brooke's was still enormously popular: today Owen is widely taken to be 'the voice' of Western Front disillusionment while Brooke's poetry is out of fashion.[2]

Although there was certainly a remarkable outpouring of war literature in the late 1920s and early 1930s which sought to tell 'the truth about the war' more frankly than had been possible in the post-war decade, even a brief amount of reading will show that very few writers were 'anti-war' in the fullest sense of opposing Britain's role, asserting that victory was not worth winning or expressing shame at their involvement. In reality, as we might expect from a nation so profoundly and widely affected by the war effort and by casualties, readers consistently preferred literature (and especially novels) whose themes and 'messages' were positive and uplifting. As Rosa M. Bracco has shown in her pioneering study *Merchants of Hope*, middlebrow, best-selling authors provided a sense of continuity, reassurance, consolation and pride in the war effort.[3] Nor were romantic and sentimental bestsellers such as Ernest Raymond's

Tell England (1922) confined to the immediate post-war years. In fact 'book for book, the British public over a thirty-year period (i.e., from the beginning of the 1920s to the end of the 1940s), seem to have preferred the patriotic to the disenchanted type of war book'.[4] Literary critics have too often focused on enduring literary merit to the neglect of the more ephemeral popularity of competent middlebrow writers. Nor is it safe to take titles at face value. For example, C. E. Montague's *Disenchantment* (1922) might seem to provide the perfect *leitmotiv* for the decade, but the author immediately regretted the title as too sweeping and misleading. Montague, a distinguished journalist and liberal idealist aged forty-seven in 1914, had dyed his grey hair and lied about his age in order to serve. He remained intensely patriotic and proud of Manchester's contribution to victory, but regretted the loss of idealism during the war, the harsh terms of the peace with Germany and the cynical atmosphere in post-war England.[5]

With one or two exceptions, to be discussed later, it should not surprise us that the ideas expressed in war literature (often with memoirs covering pre-war and post-war experience as well as the war years), were usually complex and even contradictory. Some intellectuals who later recalled the war mainly in terms of horror, fear and brutalization also experienced it as an opportunity, a privilege and a revelation. Indeed 'ambivalence towards the war is the main characteristic of the best and most honest of the war literature'.

> The same men who cried out at the inhumanity of the war often confessed that they had loved it with a passion and wondered if they would ever be able to free themselves from the front's magic spell.[6]

A good example of an outstanding work of memoir-fiction impossible to categorize as pro- or anti-war is Frederic

Manning's *The Middle Parts of Fortune* (1930). Despite his personal inadequacies as a private and eventually a sub-altern (notably alcoholism), Manning conveys the idea of combat as a supreme test of character in which those who come through achieve a lasting sense of liberation and self-knowledge. As Cyril Falls remarked when the book was published (in a bowdlerized version as *Her Privates We*), 'Here indeed are the authentic British infantrymen. Other books cause you to wonder how we won the war . . . this one helps one to understand that we could not have lost it.'[7]

Manning's work exemplifies a wider issue, namely that realistic descriptions of the horrors of combat and other negative aspects of military experience do not necessarily entail an overall anti-war stance. This is an obvious point yet it is often overlooked. Hugh Cecil has shown, in his excellent study *The Flower of Battle*, that some of the bestselling authors of the period, such as Wilfred Ewart, Gilbert Frankau, Ronald Gurner and Richard Blaker combined a harsh picture of army life and horrific evocations of combat with a positive, uplifting message. Even an overtly bitter 'anti-war' novel such as Richard Aldington's *Death of a Hero* (1929) evinced pride in the endurance of ordinary soldiers, admiration for heroism, and faith in the high command.[8]

In my contribution to *Facing Armageddon* I have already published my ideas about the difficulties of defining what it meant to be 'anti-war' in the 1920s, and, consequently, need only recapitulate the main points here. In an obvious sense, virtually everyone was 'anti-war' in not wishing to see another conflict like that of 1914–18. Britain produced no exultant warrior-nationalist like Ernst Jünger ('one feels that Jünger is a danger to society, but cannot resist liking and admiring him personally', wrote Cyril Falls), although Alfred Pollard, VC runs him close.[9] Clearly many of the best-known writers (including Robert Graves, Aldington and Herbert Read) were striving to get the war 'out of their systems' and banish nightmares, hence Graves's very apt title – *Goodbye To All That*. They were certainly not aspiring to be historians or scholars. Some writers 'looked back in anger' to pre-war British society, whereas others, such as Aldington and Oliver Onions, were more embittered by post-war experience. Siegfried Sassoon directed his most splenetic tirades against ignorance and complacency on the home front during the war, including shirkers, strikers and especially women. Graves frankly admitted in 1930 that he had deliberately mixed and spiced up all the incidents he could think of to produce a bestseller because he desperately needed the money.[10]

The paradox has long been recognized that some of the angriest anti-war satirists were not pacifists or conscientious objectors, but brave, efficient and even zealous subalterns such as Sassoon (a notable killer), Graves and Owen who voluntarily returned to the front after recovering from wounds or illness. Herbert Read, despite his anarchist views, has even been compared to Jünger for his warrior qualities. Indeed, it has been argued that these writers were not anti-war at all in the conventional sense.[11] A large element of their mental turmoil, frustration and anger was due to sexual problems deriving from their education and repressive home environment. Their combat experience, at worst, only exacerbated existing hang-ups. More positively they *needed the war* to obtain personal freedom and to seek love and consolation through suffering. Though justifiably angry at some aspects of the war (such as inept staff work which appeared to be directly responsible for the deaths of comrades), and even more at wartime propaganda and the disappointments of the post-war world, they remained proud of their regiments and personal achievements, and deeply grateful for the unique experience of comradeship. For example, Guy Chapman, a humane scholar and certainly no militarist, reflected towards the end of his life: 'To the years between 1914 and 1918 I owe everything of lasting value in my make-up. For any cost I paid in physical and mental vigour they gave me back a supreme fulfilment I should never otherwise have had.' Anthony Eden, an exceptionally brave officer, similarly recalled: 'I had entered the holocaust still childish and I emerged tempered by my experience, but with my illusions intact, neither shattered nor cynical.'[12]

The publishing boom in books which emphasized negative aspects of the war – mud, blood and futility – provoked an immediate counter-attack from former officers with a better sense of historical perspective. Just after the war, for example, Charles Carrington had written a plain, factual account of his combat experience, which included some of the fiercist fighting in 1916 and 1917, but he did not publish it until 1929, under the pseudonym Charles Edmonds (as *A Subaltern's War*), expressly to offset the current emotional, pessimistic trend. He and his fellow volunteers were not 'disenchanted' because they had known from the outset that they faced a terrible ordeal, but were determined to see it through to a victorious conclusion. There was no alternative for an honest, patriotic citizen. In an eloquent epilogue he challenged the caricature of front-line experience as one of unrelieved suffering, fear and deprivation. Such accounts denied both the soldier's capacity for an inner life and also for moments of intense happiness despite, or perhaps because of, appalling physical conditions. David Kelly, later a distinguished diplomat, was another former infantry officer who did not recognize the brave and patient troops he had served with in the travesty conveyed by the debunking 'war books'. In *Thirty-Nine Months with 'The Tigers'* (1930) he sought to depict 'the real atmosphere of our Army': the fighting troops did not pretend to enjoy the war but never questioned its necessity. They realized well enough the mistakes of superior authority but accepted them as inevitable. There was a complete absence of heroics.[13]

The most combative riposte to the stream of anti-war literature was Douglas Jerrold's polemical booklet *The Lie About The War*, published in February 1930. The author, a well-known writer and publisher, had lost an arm serving with the Royal Naval Division, whose official history he had written. In reviewing sixteen recent war books, Jerrold argued that although the war had been tragic it had also yielded positive political results, while even for individuals its effects were by no means all negative. Perhaps his most important point was that war is *par excellence* a struggle between large, disciplined groups. The authors under review ignored the wider purposes and meaning of the war by focusing on individual experience.

Jerrold's critique received support from his fellow official historian, Cyril Falls, whose much more comprehensive and balanced review *War Books* (1930) still commands a good deal of respect from military historians today. Falls disliked books which pandered to a lust for horror, brutality and filth; he was appalled at the constant belittlement of motives, of intelligence and of zeal. The most misleading evidence, he believed, was produced by telescoping scenes and events which in themselves might be true. Thus

> Every sector becomes a bad one, every working party is shot to pieces; if a man is killed or wounded his brains or his entrails always protrude from his body; no one ever seems to have a rest . . . Attacks succeed one another with lightning rapidity. The soldier is represented as a depressed and mournful spectre helplessly wandering about until death brought his miseries to an end.[14]

Furthermore, two celebrated authors of the time, Robert Graves and R. C. Sherriff, strongly resented being classed as 'anti-war'. Graves expressed surprise at being acclaimed

as the author of a 'vivid treatise against war': he was indeed
saying goodbye to *all that*, including the stuffy conventions
of pre-war society, wartime hysteria and personal problems
at the time of writing, including a marital breakdown and
being grilled by the police on suspicion of attempted murder. Although critical of some regular officers' snobbery,
Graves was extremely proud of serving with the Royal
Welch Fusiliers and remained so throughout his life. On
3 September 1939 he would again volunteer for infantry
service but was deemed unfit. In his sequel *But It Still Goes
On* (1930), he responded seriously to criticism about errors
of detail, but remarked, sensibly, that the criterion of strict
accuracy was only applicable to military histories. Mixing
up dates was inevitable for a writer in his circumstances:
'high explosive barrages will make a liar or visionary of
anyone'. He also remarked perceptively that 'propaganda
novels' can only be assessed on their own terms: 'as propaganda they are all the more effective in that they are not
dated records but dramatic generalisations'.[15]

The other individual rebuttal of association with 'anti-
war sentiments' may be more surprising. R. C. Sherriff's
Journey's End has long occupied such a key position in the
myth of anti-war literature that it comes as quite a shock to
discover (notably from R. M. Bracco) that this was entirely
at odds with the dramatist's intention, not only when the
play made its amazingly popular debut in 1929, but for the
whole of his life. The origins of this ambivalence lay in
the complete contrast in outlooks between Sherriff and his
first producer, Maurice Browne. Sherriff's career had been
transformed for the better when he was commissioned into
the 9th Battalion of the East Surrey Regiment and saw active service in France. Like Graves he remained extremely
proud of his regiment and the comradeship he found there.
By contrast Browne was a pacifist and a conscientious ob-
jector who had remained in the United States throughout

the war. Sherriff would later write that his characters were 'simple, unquestioning men who fought the war because it seemed the only right and proper thing to do . . . [it was a play] in which not a word was spoken against the war . . . and no word of condemnation was uttered'. When the first reviews appeared in 1929 Sherriff had protested that he had not tried to point any kind of moral; he had merely wished to perpetuate the memory of some of the men he had known.[16] Sherriff's intentions had been to stress the virtues of duty and perseverance in the face of fear and extreme danger, but in the long run, as Bracco shows, these ideas could not prevail over the play's claustrophobic setting in a trench and the deaths in action of all the main characters.

So far I have argued that the war literature of the 1920s was full of ambiguities and could not, taken as a whole, be held to support the 'anti-war' myth. But this is not to suggest that were no true anti-war writers or that the myth lacked literary foundations.[17] One book in particular exerted a phenomenal international appeal and is still often cited as 'the book' about the war. Erich Maria Remarque's *All Quiet On the Western Front* was published in book form in Germany in January 1929, preceded by a unique advertising campaign. It sold one million copies in Germany alone in the first year. It was translated into some twenty languages including Chinese and Esperanto. An excellent English translation (by an Australian scholar A. W. Wheen) appeared as early as March 1929.[18] Remarque's amazing success opened the floodgates to a spate of war books on what had recently appeared to be a topic of waning public interest.[19] Reviews were sharply divided. Most were ecstatic on the grounds that *All Quiet on the Western Front* 'told the truth about the war', it was 'the greatest of all war books', and it was 'the Bible of the common soldier'. Critics, on the other hand, described it as mere propaganda. They dwelt on the author's apparent obsession with latrines, food and mangled bodies.

This was to underrate Remarque's appeal to the ordinary reader. True, his style is basic and lacking in delicacy, but the book seems to have been written in a surge of emotion that still exerts a compulsive appeal. A succession of brief, dramatic incidents with a minimum of distracting detail grips one's attention. There are poignant scenes such as the narrator's leave-taking of his dying mother, his encounter with starving Russian prisoners of war and the pathetic death of a comrade in hospital whose boots are much sought after. The message is brutally clear:

> It must be all lies and of no account when the culture of a thousand years could not prevent this stream of blood being poured out, these torture-chambers in their hundreds of thousands. A hospital alone shows what war is.
>
> I am young ... yet I know nothing of life but despair, death, fear, and fatuous superficiality cast over an abyss of sorrow.[20]

Mystery still cloaks Remarque's early life and brief military service. Whereas the characters in the book are portrayed as disillusioned volunteers, Remarque was conscripted in November 1916. He probably experienced front-line conditions in Flanders for a few weeks in mid-1917 and was wounded. After several post-war years as a ne'er-do-well he hit upon the idea of the war as the sole cause of his own and his generation's malaise. Modris Eksteins has argued persuasively that *All Quiet on the Western Front* is not a war memoir and, indeed, is not really about the events of the war (it is noticeably thin on details of dates, places and units): rather it is an angry statement about the effects of war on the author and his comrades. In this stark, relentless narrative the characters are merely victims. This portrayal of tormented and degraded soldiers is what one might expect from an unwilling conscript thrown into the hell of the Ypres sector late in the war, where food was scarce, living conditions appalling and defeat impending. Eksteins concludes that *All Quiet on the Western Front* was not so much 'the truth about the war' as, first and foremost, the truth about Erich Maria Remarque in 1928. But as he wisely adds, other writers were also using the war for their own purposes. 'The war boom of the late twenties reflected less a genuine interest in the war than a perplexed international commiseration.'[21]

All Quiet on the Western Front was published at a critical turning point in what proved to be the 'inter-war' period. 1929 marked the tenth anniversary of the Treaty of Versailles and was a year of mounting economic crisis culminating in the Great Depression. In Britain, Remarque's portrayal of German soldiers as miserable, downtrodden victims of an unnecessary and meaningless war met with some sympathy. Like Henri Barbusse earlier, Remarque had struck the right note: his soldiers were mere cannon-fodder who could have been members of any army. By suggesting that the Germans were not militarists after all, Remarque was contributing at a popular level to undermining the notion of a collective German war guilt. Was his novel 'more influential than political and historical revisionism'? Eksteins suggests extravagantly that he alone 'accomplished much more than all the revisionist historians in America and Europe put together'.[22]

All Quiet on the Western Front was made into a hugely successful film by Lewis Milestone in the United States and released in May 1930. It was to prove even more controversial than the book, especially in Germany, where early showings were disrupted by Nazi thugs, and it was banned for a time because of its malicious depiction of the German army and the Nation's defeat. The film faithfully captured the spirit of the book, perhaps even enhancing it by a stricter attention to chronology, and by the brilliant idea of transposing the butterfly incident to the final scene (from page 142 in the English translation) as the direct cause of Paul Bäumer's death. The film was an immediate hit in New York, London and Paris. It was widely labelled 'the greatest of all war films', as demonstrating the madness of war and the futility of patriotism and materialism. Perhaps even more successfully than the book, the film inculcated the idea that the war had been an identical and equally disastrous experience for all soldiers and all armies.[23]

In Britain, however, it should be remembered that, throughout the inter-war period, as Michael Paris has shown, 'films which portrayed the War in traditional and patriotic terms far outnumbered those that raised even some ambiguously phrased doubts about whether such sacrifice could ever be justified'. The more common view, as borne out by cinema attendances and by the popularity of films which stressed its heroic and sacrificial nature, was that the war had been justified as 'another bloody but glorious page in the history of the British Empire'. This was particularly true of the series of popular documentary dramas produced by British Instructional Films (BIF) in the 1920s. The screen versions of battles such as Mons, Ypres and the Somme presented 'sanitised, heroic images, testaments to courage, patriotism and the nobility of sacrifice'.[24] These films told essentially the same story as popular fiction of the period.

In his recent survey of British war films, Michael Paris shows that even in the 1930s cinematic reconstructions of the First World War were either ambiguous in their message or portrayed the war as straightforward adventure. For example, the film of *Journey's End*, released in 1930, remains as controversial as the play. Critics continue to regard it as an indictment of war but, as R. C. Sherriff insisted, it should also be seen as a film about duty and endurance. The war exists and Englishmen must see it through to the end. Paris echoes my argument when he writes:

> British cinema had generally been reluctant to portray the war as unmitigated disaster and had adopted a far less critical approach.
>
> [The truly negative interpretation of the First World War] really only took hold of the popular imagination during the 1960s when a flood of revisionist popular histories, novels, documentaries and films was created to mark the fiftieth anniversaries of the conflict.[25]

In his precisely titled study *A War Imagined: the First World War and English Culture*, Samuel Hynes surveys a very wide range of literature before reaching the conclusions given in his final chapter 'The War Becomes Myth'. Very fairly he details the historical criticisms mentioned in this chapter, but once the war experience has been transformed into 'myth' then, for him, this notion takes on a cultural reality of its own impervious to historical *caveats* or objections. He clearly understands why this process is deplored by military historians and generals:

> It was not simply that in that version the war was bloody and cruel; it was that it was meaningless. If the myth-making authors of those books were right, then the war had no history, in the sense of a story expressing the meaning of events, but was anti-historical, apocalyptic, an incoherence, a gap in time.
>
> The Myth accomplished this demolition of meaning, as Jerrold acutely observed, by telling the story of the war not in the traditional way – that is, in terms of the big battalions – but through the stories of individuals, and

obscure ones at that: junior officers and men in the ranks. But to the individual personally Jerrold wrote, 'all operations of war are meaningless and futile'.[26]

Modris Eksteins reaches a similarly dismal conclusion from a historian's standpoint. If the war could have meaning only at the level of individual experience, and particularly of individual suffering, then it could only be approached through literature and art, not history. He elaborates on the twentieth century as an anti-historical age of disintegration in which historians have struggled vainly against the odds to make sense of great events. In particular, he asserts that historians have failed to find explanations for the war that correspond to the horrendous realities, whereas Remarque did so, and, virtually overnight, became the bestseller of all previous time.[27]

Eksteins is surely right about the ascendancy of the literary over historical interpretations of the war in the 1920s and 1930s. Historians were confronted not only with the almost total lack of official documents, but also with the virtually impossible problem of putting these kaleidoscopic events into perspective while they were still in a state of flux.

However, from the present perspective, historians should not merely challenge Eksteins's pessimistic determinism, but also demonstrate that their interpretations of the war are of wider significance than literary ones precisely because they seek to answer the larger questions about politics, strategy and the effects of war on international relations. I believe moreover, that they have been doing this successfully for some time – an issue I shall return to in my concluding chapter.

It should not surprise us that early attempts to write the history of the war, in the two most important cases developing or adapting wartime publications, displayed traditional, patriotic and even romantic values similar to

those of the bestselling war fiction and memoirs. A vital
consideration was that – except for the actions of a few
ex-Cabinet ministers who bent or flouted the rules – official political and military documents were not available.[28]
The volumes of the Official History were slow to appear
and were presented in such a dense format as to be impenetrable to all but the most dedicated students or high-
level participants anxious to discover how they had been
portrayed.

Sir Arthur Conan Doyle's massive history *The British
Campaign in France and Flanders* (six volumes, 1916–20)
did not cope well with the problems of documentation and
perspective, and signally failed to achieve the lasting validity which he expected. Given his literary fame, as the
creator of Sherlock Holmes, and his profound belief in the
justice of British military policy, he was frustrated by being
denied access to official material during the war, and even
suffered rebuffs from generals he approached privately. He
adopted a narrow concept of operational writing, largely
ignoring such important considerations as staff work, logistics and aerial warfare, in order to focus on the progress
of individual brigades and divisions. No reviewer accused
him of getting a brigade or a battalion out of place, but this
was a modest achievement. After the war Conan Doyle did
not deliberately continue his writing in a spirit of wartime
propaganda, but he found it impossible to change his optimistic tone and obsolete methods of describing operations.
Within a decade his work was no longer referred to by a new
generation of historians but, as a recent reappraisal gener-
ously concludes, 'in the aftermath of war [his] work had a
relevance to the society for which it was written'.[29]

John Buchan was as patriotic as Conan Doyle and in temperament even more romantic, but he had had the advantage of serving at Haig's general headquarters in 1916. In
February 1917 he was brought back to London to head the

Department of Information (later the independent Ministry of Information with Buchan as its deputy head). Buchan also performed the herculean labour of writing the bulk of *Nelson's History of the War*. This work he revised and re-published in four volumes as *A History of the Great War* in 1921–22. Buchan's statement of faith in the purpose of the British war effort made his history a commemorative and still confident monument to the recent conflict. The themes which most interested Buchan were those of histor-ical perspective, the righteousness of Britain's cause, and a continuing role for 'great captains', even in the siege con-ditions of the Western Front. A confirmed 'Westerner', he became and remained a life-long admirer and supporter of Sir Douglas Haig, but this did not inhibit him from mak-ing sharp criticisms of the Passchendaele campaign and of the Cambrai operation which followed it. Apart from his former chief, Lord Milner, he found no political equiva-lents of the Army's 'great captains' in Whitehall. Despite his personal observations of combat on the Western Front, Buchan's character 'constantly tempted him towards ro-mance'. In his *History* he had uneasily juxtaposed carnage and pastoral romance but without a trace of the irony so eagerly sought by Paul Fussell and other modern cultural critics. Nevertheless, despite his limitations in outlook and range of sources, Buchan wrote history as distinct from pro-paganda. His volumes made a significant contribution to the early historical shaping and assessment of the war, and both C. R. M. F. Cruttwell and Basil Liddell Hart took his work seriously.[30] The latter in particular owed a great deal to Buchan in establishing his own career after 1918, and like him continued to stress the importance of the 'great captain' in twentieth-century warfare.

Of the third multi-volume historian of the war to be considered here, Arthur Balfour mischievously remarked, 'Winston has written his war memoirs and called it

The World Crisis'. This witticism was accurate in that Churchill concentrated heavily on those aspects of the war in which he had been personally involved, including the Antwerp operation in 1914, the development of the tank, the supply of munitions and, above all, Gallipoli. Yet, as modern scholars acknowledge, Churchill's profound interest in the study and writing of military history were already abundantly evident in his concern to cover 'the other side of the hill', in his attempt to base controversial judgements on the best available evidence, as in his celebrated analysis of comparative casualty statistics, and not least in consulting a variety of differing viewpoints, including, most daringly, Douglas Haig's for the operations on the Western Front in 1918.[31]

The World Crisis, published in six volumes between 1923 and 1929, made an enormous impact, due not simply to the author's important role in the war and his majestic style, but also because he made extensive use of official documents not generally available to historians until the mid-1960s. Consequently Churchill's volumes and other books by 'insiders' were frequently quarried by other historians. Some of the volumes were serialized in leading newspapers, including *The Times*, and there have been several abridged versions, including a two-volume edition in 1938 and a single-volume edition first published in 1931 and reissued in paperback in 1960. These and other popular war memoirs were also purchased by the leading circulating libraries, thus greatly expanding the number of readers beyond the total of books sold. With additional American advances Churchill received £27,000 for his first volume before a single copy had been sold. The second volume enabled him to complete work on his home at Chartwell, while still leaving him well in credit.[32]

Churchill was fiercely critical of the Entente's strategy of attrition on the Western Front and argued persuasively, from his analysis of casualty statistics ('The Blood Count'), that Britain and France had consistently suffered more severely than Germany. But he somewhat weakened his argument by stressing that it was the failure at Gallipoli that had made the Entente's offensives necessary. Although he included a laudatory pen-portrait of Haig, he concluded that the campaign of 1916 on the Western Front was 'from beginning to end a welter of slaughter which . . . left the British and French armies weaker in relation to the Germans than when it opened'. Apart from relieving pressure on Verdun, 'no strategical advantages of any kind had been gained'. Third Ypres was described as 'a sombre experiment that had failed disastrously', though for this he blamed the Chief of Imperial General Staff (CIGS), General Sir William Robertson, rather than Haig. Regarding the start of the final victorious Allied advance from August 1918, Churchill wrote that Haig and Foch 'had year after year conducted with obstinacy and serene confidence offensives which we now know to have been as hopeless as they were disastrous'. But in 1918, with the Germans weakened by their own offensives and the arrival of the Americans in large numbers, conditions had changed, making mobile operations again possible. Thus both Haig and Foch 'were vindicated in the end'. He concluded with a fulsome tribute to the British Army and the national war effort, and listed achievements (in 1918) 'which will excite the wonder of future generations'.[33]

Although Churchill's *The World Crisis* was less overtly anti-military than Lloyd George's memoirs, published later in the 1930s, and qualified its critical remarks on Haig, it nevertheless constituted a powerful indictment of the high command and of British strategy in the main war theatre: the great offensives of 1916 and 1917 were described as futile and profligate with soldiers' lives; the generals were depicted as reactionary in their attitude to tanks (in Churchill's partisan view a war-winning weapon); and, above all, his powerful analysis of casualty statistics provided evidence for generations of critics that Haig's attritional strategy had been misconceived and was ultimately counter-productive.[34]

In the 1920s there emerged a new generation of military historians, nearly all ex-officers with combat experience in the First World War, whose attitudes towards British strategy, tactics, generalship and staff work were generally critical, in some cases openly hostile.

The two military critics and historians who dominated the inter-war scene were Major-General J. F. C. Fuller and Captain B. H. Liddell Hart. As a convalescent subaltern in 1916 Liddell Hart had written a fulsome eulogy of the British high command and staff, but by the 1930s his views had swung full circle and he became sharply critical, especially of Haig and Robertson. His (and Fuller's) plausible defence of their critical stance was that more could be learnt from defeats than victories, coupled with anxiety that the Army hierarchy had learnt nothing and would repeat the bloodbaths of the Somme and Passchendaele in a future war. Fuller became particularly sarcastic and intemperate, for example remarking of one despised general who had been awarded the GCB (Grand Cross of the Order of the Bath) that the initials must stand for 'Great Cretin Brotherhood'. As critics of the inter-war Army many of their shots were probably on target, but as influential historians of the First World War their approach was too polemical.[35]

They were tremendously successful in creating a historical 'myth' regarding Britain's role in the war comparable to the literary 'myth' discussed earlier, several aspects of which are still influential today. Liddell Hart, more especially, advanced the seductive theories that Britain could and should have avoided total commitment to mass continental warfare, and that Germany had been defeated by the naval blockade and internal collapse rather than by the wasteful attrition on the Western Front. He abetted Churchill's case that a strategy of indirect approach, which was attempted and failed tragically at the Dardanelles, was the correct course for Britain. Additionally he helped to focus attention on the Palestine campaign and the romantic exploits of T. E. Lawrence as an alternative to the bloodbath in Flanders.[36]

The work which surely did most damage to the generals and the conduct of the war on the Western Front – thus powerfully endorsing the literary myth – was Lloyd George's *Memoirs*, published in six volumes between 1933 and 1936. In his foreword to the new, two-volume, edition in 1938 Lloyd George wrote:

> I aim to tell the naked truth about the war as I saw it from the conning-tower at Downing Street. I saw how the incredible heroism of the common man was being squandered to repair the incompetence of the trained inexperts [sic] . . . in the narrow, selfish and unimaginative strategy and in the ghastly butchery of a succession of vain and insane offensives.

It is perhaps unnecessary to comment that Lloyd George had been prime minister while the most controversial of these offensives had taken place and had the constitutional responsibility to stop it if he deemed it to be failing or too costly in casualties. In his original preface he had referred to 'reckless and unintelligent handling [which] brought us almost to the rim of catastrophe, and how we were saved largely by the incredible folly of our foes'. He regretted 'more than words can express the necessity for telling the bare facts of our bloodstained stagger to victory'. Lloyd George, with Liddell Hart's help, devoted a special effort to the prosecution case in the Passchendaele campaign because he saw this as crucial in shaping the British people's memory of the Great War. Aware that he might be criticized

for seeking to demolish the reputation of Field Marshal Earl
Haig after his death (in 1928), Lloyd George added a chapter on 'Lord Haig's Diaries and After', where he argued that
Alfred Duff Cooper's two-volume biography of the former
commander-in-chief (1935–6), which had quoted 'remarkably sterile and undistinguished' extracts from Haig's diaries, demanded a response.[37] Lloyd George's immediate
target may have been Duff Cooper, but the real objective
of his venom was Haig. The latter has five closely printed
columns of entries in the index, nearly all of them uncom-
plimentary to say the least. Here is a sample:

> His reputation founded on cavalry exploits.
> Insists on premature use of tanks.
> His refusal to face unpleasant facts.
> His limited vision.
> Viciously resists Lloyd George's attempts to get
>   Unity of Command.
> His stubborn mind transfixed on the Somme.
> Prefers to gamble with men's lives rather than to
>   admit an error.
> Completely ignorant of the state of ground at
>   Passchendaele.
> Painstaking but unimaginative.
> Narrowness of his outlook.
> Incapable of changing his plans.
> His liking for great offensives.
> Unequal to his task.
> Did not inspire his men.
> His ingenuity at shifting the blame to other
>   shoulders than his own.
> Only took part in two battles during the war.

So it is clear that the prime minister was not wholly satis-
fied with his commander-in-chief! But note also two further
entries:

> Lloyd George had no personal quarrel with . . . [and]
> No conspicuous officer better qualified for highest
> command than.

One should also not miss the index entries on 'military mind' which include:

> Military mind, narrowness of.
> Stubbornness of, not peculiar to America.
> Does not seem to understand arithmetic.
> Represented by Sir Henry Wilson's fantastic
>   memorandum.
> Obsessed with the North-West Frontier of India.
> Impossibility of trusting.
> Regards thinking as a form of mutiny.[38]

Lloyd George's *Memoirs* fanned the flames of bitter controversy. Although Haig's supporters, including two generals, Maurice and Gwynn, rallied to his defence, most reviewers favoured the former prime minister's interpretation. As much as any historical source these *Memoirs* 'stigmatized indelibly' the military elite in the popular memory.[39]

At the outset I mentioned Correlli Barnett's charge that the anti-war literature of the late 1920s had fatally undermined British confidence in the national achievement in the First World War, thereby contributing to a reluctance to rearm when confronted by the Nazi threat in the 1930s, and leading ultimately to the 'collapse of British power'. I believe that this was one important element in the appeasing mentality, though only entertained by a small minority of the population as a whole. I have suggested, from a longer perspective, that – with all its complexities and ambiguities – British anti-war literature, given an enormous boost by the book and film *All Quiet on the Western Front*, had laid the foundation of the Myth which has been summarized by Samuel Hynes as follows:

the idealism betrayed; the early high-mindedness that
turned in mid-war to bitterness and cynicism; the growing
feeling among soldiers of alienation from the people at
home for whom they were fighting; the rising resentment
of politicians and profiteers and ignorant, patriotic
women; the growing sympathy for the men on the other
side, betrayed in the same ways and suffering the same
hardships; the emerging sense of the war as a machine and
of all soldiers as its victims; the bitter conviction that the
men in the trenches fought for no cause, in a war that
could not be stopped.[40]

Moreover, where military historians had struggled with
little success to present the conflict in an intellectual frame-
work and a language which would appeal to a readership
inclined to say 'goodbye to all that', Winston Churchill
and, more especially, Lloyd George had published powerful, scintillating, and seemingly authoritative *Memoirs* sad-
dling the generals with the chief responsibility for the incompetent conduct of the war and the enormous butcher's
bill. These notions, which I would term the literary myth
and the political myth, would excite the attention of a new
generation in a very different military, social and cultural
atmosphere in the 1960s. This will form the subject of my
third chapter.

3 Donkeys and Flanders mud
the war rediscovered in the 1960s

My thesis in this chapter is that at the end of the twentieth century popular notions of the First World War in general, and Britain's role in particular, were largely shaped in the 1960s, in part reflecting the very different concerns and political issues of that turbulent decade, but in part resurrecting 'anti-war' beliefs of the 1930s.

At the risk of over-simplification and distortion, these are some of the main events that provide the context in which a new generation was introduced to the history of the First World War. There was, first and foremost, a pervasive fear of all-out nuclear war which is hard to imagine now. The Campaign for Nuclear Disarmament and its annual Aldermaston march reached a peak of popularity and media attention in the late 1950s and early 1960s. The Cuban missile crisis in 1962 provided hard evidence that the world had teetered on the brink of annihilation. National service was ended in 1960 so the last conscripts had left the armed forces by 1963. Thus ended a system of compulsory service, reintroduced in 1939, by which the majority of the male population – for good or ill – at the very least had some familiarity with the realities of military life. By the end of the decade this was ceasing to be so, and the gap has necessarily grown ever wider. Not that unfamiliarity with army life has entailed a diminishing interest in military history, in fact quite the contrary.

The 1960s were also notable for the emergence of an independent youth culture and of much greater freedom in sexual matters. Already, in 1957, the Wolfenden Committee had reported in favour of legalizing homosexual relations between consenting adults in private, while in 1960 the outcome of the 'Lady Chatterley' trial heralded a new and more liberal era for the publication and discussion of formerly 'taboo' topics. As Philip Larkin would wistfully recall in his poem 'Annus Mirabilis':

> Sexual intercourse began
> In nineteen sixty-three
> (Which was rather late for me) -
> Between the end of the *Chatterley* ban
> And the Beatles' first LP.[1]

This year (1963) was also that of the Profumo scandal, in which the Secretary of State for War had consorted with expensive call-girls whose circle included Stephen Ward, a society osteopath, and Captain Eugene Ivanov, naval attaché at the Russian Embassy. This affair had all the ingredients to titillate the popular press: sleaze and hypocrisy in the Tory Party and high society with the possibility of espionage. John Profumo's political career was ruined and Stephen Ward committed suicide, whereas Christine Keeler and Mandy Rice Davies became celebrities. As Arthur Marwick commented:

> It also provided a magnificent peg upon which to hang denunciations of Britain's moral decadence.[2]

The increasingly dire plight of the US forces in the Vietnamese civil war provided a focus for anti-American, anti-imperial, anti-military and anti-authority radical protest. It became, in Arthur Marwick's phrase, 'the great universal issue'. The rapidity and scale of the build-up of US troops in Vietnam gives a good indication of the growing desperation in Washington to end the war by victory through overwhelming numerical and material strength. By the end of 1961 there were some 3,000 US personnel in South Vietnam; four years later the number had risen to 181,000 and by 1966 to 385,000. In 1968 the communist 'Tet' offensives against southern cities were defeated, but so unpopular was the war that US President Lyndon Johnson decided not to seek re-election and to begin peace negotiations. In January 1969 US troops in Vietnam reached a peak of 541,000, and thereafter there was an equally rapid withdrawal until the last personnel left in March 1973.[3]

Radical student protest and rebellion culminated in violent demonstrations and clashes with the police in Paris and other European cities. A *Daily Express* headline of 23 October 1967 neatly captured the irony of the situation: 'Mobs howling for peace in Vietnam warred with Police'. Britain had no equivalent of the extremist Baader-Meinhof Gang (whose leaders were eventually arrested in 1972), but university lectures and administration were disrupted at the London School of Economics (LSE) and on other campuses. At the LSE the initial cause of unrest was the appointment of a new director with Rhodesian connections and believed to be associated with the apartheid regime in South Africa, but student power became a wider issue. The college was briefly closed and 'a thoroughly embittered and poisoned atmosphere was created, with much vandalism'. Even at the conservative and largely apolitical King's College London we were concerned that departmental signs

indicating 'War Studies' and 'Military Studies' would provoke hostile demonstrations, but all remained quiet on the
Strand front. However, at Field Marshal Haig's former
Oxford college, Brasenose, his portrait in the hall was given
a new caption 'Murderer of One Million Men', while the
war memorial at the college entrance was removed and
never replaced.[4]

Lastly, the declining national significance of Armistice
Day truly reflected uncertainty, apathy and even hostility
towards the annual commemoration of those who had lost
their lives in Britain's twentieth-century conflicts, and especially in the First World War. Already, in the 1950s, with
the Armistice commemoration moved from 11 November
to the nearest Sunday, the profound significance of the two
minutes' silence had been reduced. Now it was observed
only as a part of a church service or in ceremonies at the
Cenotaph in Whitehall and at local war memorials. In the
1960s Armistice Day 'slid into disrepute as the war which
had originated it slid into disrepute, as a war in which, it
was alleged, the young were cynically misled and slaugh-
tered by the old'. This decline continued through the 1970s
as the survivors and close relatives of 'the fallen' inevitably
dwindled in number. Apart from the Royal British Legion
and veterans of both world wars, liberal opinion inclined
to the view that the First World War 'had all been futile
and a waste, and that all should be ashamed of it'. That war
should not be commemorated because to do so would imply
a respect for events which a more enlightened generation
could not give.[5]

In sum, after the humiliating fiasco of Suez in 1956
and with the growing opposition to US intervention in
Vietnam, the 1960s was in some respects a very unpropi-
tious decade for the study of military history, with the First
World War in particular widely perceived as the epitome of
cynical, incompetent leadership, horror, needless sacrifice
and futility.

Yet the decade also witnessed a remarkable revival of interest in the First World War which can be traced to two related causes. First, and negatively, the post-1945 'battle of the memoirs' of leading participants in the Second World War seemed to be played out – although for scholars it could be said that this vast subject was only just opening up. Publishers and authors sensed that there was once again a popular market for books on the earlier war. Alan Moorehead's *Gallipoli* (1956) was an early example of a lively, critical and emotionally charged narrative which would appeal to a new generation who had more recently experienced combat, or at least seen military service.

But a far more positive stimulus was provided by the prospect of the fiftieth anniversaries falling between 1964 and 1968, accompanied by the realization that the generation of First World War veterans was rapidly 'fading away' and that their story had remained largely untold – squeezed out between the subalterns' poetry and literary recollections on the one hand and the disputes between 'frocks' and 'brasshats' on the other. A further consideration was that the range of sources available – documentary and others – had vastly expanded since the 1930s, for example in the collections at the Imperial War Museum and in numerous local and regimental museums. Official documents, such as Cabinet and War Office papers, should also, in principle, have been released from 1964 onwards under the 'fifty-year rule', but they do not seem to have been used much, if at all, by military historians during the 1960s.

A new era dawned in 1967, when the Public Records Act reduced from fifty to thirty years the delay in releasing official government papers to public inspection.[6] Consequently, although some sensitive collections were withheld, records relating to the First World War and the inter-war period became generally accessible in 1968. Few scholars immediately availed themselves of this indispensable source, or of the many private collections released by the 'thaw', but in the 1970s and 1980s there would truly be a new era or watershed in the historiography of the First World War.

In terms of historical perspective, however, Britain's participation in the Second World War has paradoxically made it harder to understand, and appreciate, its role in the First. A. J. P. Taylor's curious conclusion that, despite all its suffering and destruction, the Second World War was 'a good war' has gained general acceptance, particularly as applied to Britain. Only one respected historian has made a counter-claim for the greater nobility of Britain's motives and conduct in the First World War. There is superficially much to be said in defence of Taylor's judgement. The Kaiser's regime, although increasingly militaristic, was patently not such an evil force as Hitler's, and German atrocities in the First World War, greatly exaggerated in the Allied news media, were dwarfed by Nazi barbarism in the Second. Moreover Nazi Germany seemed to have posed a more direct threat to Britain's survival as an independent state, with intensive aerial bombing and rocket attacks added to the submarine menace in both wars. Only a few cynical critics would deny an element of genuine idealism in Churchill's rhetoric or of sincerity in a crusade to liberate Europe from Nazi tyranny. But this moral or idealistic component of national policy has been magnified in retrospect since the horrific discoveries at Belsen in April 1945 and the full post-war documentation of Nazi war crimes against humanity. Now the war is widely seen in terms of the Holocaust and the Allies' inadequate response to it, but at the time it was entered into and fought for similar reasons to the First World War, namely to defend Britain's independence and its empire and to prevent German domination of western Europe.

The 'exceptional' historian mentioned above is the late John Grigg, who argued in 1990 that Britain fought the

First World War in a more idealistic spirit and with a higher regard for moral values than the Second. In some ways, he suggests, the British may even have been *too* idealistic in their attitude during the First World War:

> The themes of blood sacrifice and atonement were much in evidence, but with a political twist. Britain was thought to be fighting not just to preserve its own freedom and its position in the world, but to save as well the whole human race from war itself. Those who died in the conflict were, therefore, seen as sacramental victims, purging the world of one of its worst evils.[7]

In my opinion, Grigg's arguments are persuasive as regards Britain's moral stance and conduct of the First World War, but less so in his criticisms of the Second, which include the popular targets of Unconditional Surrender and strategic bombing. What, of course, adds weight to the prevailing view is the contrasting outcome of the two world wars: in 1918 the German threat was only checked and soon reappeared in a much more menacing form, whereas in 1945 Germany was completely defeated, occupied and divided, and Nazism was effectively extirpated. Nonetheless, Grigg's arguments deserve careful attention, particularly as he stresses that the myths about the First World War were mostly created during the 1960s.

As will be made clear in the following discussion of the key works in the 1960s on the First World War, the renewed controversies on such matters as 'Easterners versus Westerners', the attrition strategy, generalship, the employment of tanks and, most problematic, casualty statistics, generated powerful emotions and even led to personal vendettas. It was almost as though the war had to be fought over again by a new generation of historians and publicists.

It is important to stress that one military historian bestrode this battle-ground – of publishing, theatre and cinema – like a colossus. Captain B. H. (from 1965 Sir Basil) Liddell Hart had attained his position of dominant influence through his immense output on the war in the 1920s and 1930s, his remarkably generous help to newcomers to the subject, and the assemblage of his enormous, unrivalled personal archives which no writer could afford to ignore.

Liddell Hart's attitude to the First World War was complex and should not be caricatured.[8] He welcomed controversy through correspondence as a way of refining his ideas, assessing the evidence and approaching 'the truth'. He remained tolerant and open-minded on many subjects related to the war and was capable, even towards the end of his life (he died in January 1970), of writing fair and balanced assessments of, for example, Sir Douglas Haig or the Allied achievement in 1918. By the 1960s, however, he was doing no new work on the First World War, being in general content to play in the arena and under the guidelines which he had done so much to establish in the inter-war period. He remained a champion of the 'indirect approach' as attempted at Gallipoli; he was sharply critical of British tactics, strategy and generalship on the Western Front; he had advised Lloyd George on the latter's war memoirs and was sympathetic to him rather than Haig; his hero was the scholar turned warrior, T. E. Lawrence. He was obsessively interested in some aspects of the war: the first battle of the Marne, the Somme, tanks, the German March 1918 offensive; but less so in others such as artillery, logistics, staff work and the eventual Allied victory. He was curiously detached from the 'real war' of the soldiers' experience. Above all, he viewed the war from the standpoint of a highly intelligent and immensely well-informed journalist with pronounced theories about tactics and strategy. These qualities made him an outstanding *critic*, but less good as a historian for whom the challenge is to empathize, understand and explain the nature of the war and how its problems were tackled. Inevitably he crossed swords with some of the new generation of military historians, notably John Terraine and Correlli Barnett. But Liddell Hart's critical stance found many admirers in the 1960s. To mention just one here, Raymond Fletcher, military commentator for *Tribune*, Labour MP for Ilkeston from 1964 to 1983, and recently unveiled as a Soviet agent, played an important part in the compilation of the entertainment *Oh What a Lovely War*. He later described his three-hour harangue to the Theatre Workshop Group on the play's message as 'one part me, one part Liddell Hart, the rest Lenin!'[9]

Leon Wolff established the fashion for the new wave of First World War histories in the 1960s with his dramatic and poignant study *In Flanders Fields* published in Britain in 1959. Professor Danchev rightly called this book 'a prototype and a portent'.[10] Wolff drew skilfully on memoirs and histories of the inter-war period to produce an attractive pastiche for a new generation of readers. He strove to produce a rounded account of the Flanders campaign of 1917 from both sides and at all levels but, as the title hinted, he was passionately convinced that the First World War was wasteful and futile. He was bitterly critical of British leadership, especially of the generals, and of Haig in particular: 'Wolff's searing description of conditions at Passchendaele introduced the horrors of the Western Front to a new generation, including myself, satiated with a decade of accounts of how Monty had beaten the Desert Fox and knocked him for six out of Africa. Wolff's anger and indignation suffused the book: the futile offensive should have been stopped but it had dragged on into November mainly due to Haig's obstinacy. The "butchers" were fair game but, by contrast, "the curs" [politicians] got off relatively lightly. Wolff tried to be fair and even-handed but his conclusion was devastating: the war had "meant nothing, solved nothing and proved nothing", and in the process had killed eight and a half million men.'[11]

Characteristically for that decade, Wolff conveyed no sense of tactical development, or what is now termed 'the learning curve', on the British side. Nor did he grapple with the meaning of 'Passchendaele' in the broader context of the war from both sides; he concluded simply that it was merely a dreadful episode in a meaningless war. It is easy to understand why Wolff's book was quarried by the compilers of *Oh What a Lovely War*.

Another military study which perhaps attracted Joan Littlewood's Theatre Workshop team even more strongly was Alan Clark's *The Donkeys* (1961), which concentrated on the BEF in the years 1914 and 1915, culminating in the ill-fated battle of Loos. Clark's epigraph of 'lions' (i.e., gallant soldiers) led by 'donkeys' (i.e., stupid generals) perfectly suited the popular radicalism of the decade. Haig, not yet Commander-in-Chief but already cast as Donkey-in-Chief, was depicted as a combination of ambition, obstinacy and megalomania. Clark maliciously suggests, for example, that Haig was more upset by King George V being thrown from his (Haig's) horse than by the tragedy of the battle of Loos. He concludes that so great was the heroism and devotion of 'the lions' that after two years of being ravaged in Haig's hopeless offensives and losing more men in a single day 'than any other army in the history of the world', they were still able to deliver victory despite all the blunders of 'the donkeys'.[12] Michael Howard found the book entertaining but 'worthless as history'.[13] This verdict, generally endorsed by serious historians, has not prevented *The Donkeys* from selling well and remaining popular. Liddell Hart had vetted Alan Clark's typescript but cannot be held responsible for its petulant tone and debunking style. Clark had faithfully followed the master's strategic view that the war could have been won in the East (i.e., at Gallipoli), but he certainly had not been Liddell Hart's pupil at university (see note 24).

In 1963, at the height of his fame as a television lecturer, journalist and historical gadfly, A. J. P. Taylor published *The First World War. An Illustrated History*. Highly popular and populist in style, it is still probably the most widely read historical work on the war as a whole in English. By 1989 it had already sold about a quarter of a million copies.[14] Taylor was deservedly famous as a historian of foreign policy and diplomacy, but had no specialist knowledge of military history. In covering this deficiency he was greatly helped by Liddell Hart, who carefully vetted his draft chapters and sent him many pages of detailed corrections and qualifications.[15] Taylor accepted and incorporated most of them but retained his own unique *persona*: penetrating, opinionated and brilliant. 'Men are reluctant to believe that great events have small causes', wrote Taylor, but he *did* believe that about the origins and course of the First World War. It had begun by accident and was pursued without any clear purpose. Victory became an end in itself: in short, the war was senseless. Taylor's mordant, laconic style was most effectively deployed in describing Third Ypres or Passchendaele:

> Failure was obvious by the end of the first day to everyone except Haig and his immediate circle. The greatest advance was less than half a mile . . . Rain fell heavily. The ground, churned up by shellfire, turned to mud. Men . . . sank up to their waists. Guns disappeared in the mud. Haig sent in tanks. These also vanished in the mud.

Taylor concluded that

> Third Ypres was the blindest slaughter of a blind war. Haig bore the greatest responsibility. Some of the

> Flanders mud sticks also to Lloyd George, the man who
> lacked the supreme authority to forbid the battle.[16]

Taylor's text sparkles with epigrams, paradoxes, hyperbole and mischief. Casual readers will be immediately struck by his ironic, irreverent, even wicked captions to the illustrations. Thus Sir John French, hurrying past civilians in court dress, is 'in training for the retreat from Mons' (page 24); Lloyd George 'casts an expert eye over munition girls' (page 63); Kitchener is photographed 'with his keeper, Sir William Robertson' (page 79); 'Haig relied on the divine help, became an earl and received £100,000 from Parliament' (page 81).[17]

But Taylor was a distinguished scholar as well as a mischievous journalist. He concluded that although the war failed to produce Utopia, 'on a more prosaic level it did rather better than most wars, though no doubt the price was excessive'. Belgium had been liberated and German domination of Europe postponed, perhaps prevented. As for the cliché that the British soldiers were 'lions led by donkeys', Taylor commented sharply that 'This character was not confined to the British, or to soldiers. All the peoples were in the same boat. The war was beyond the capacity of generals and statesmen alike'.[18]

Earlier, after thanking Liddell Hart for his great help with the book, Taylor had written: 'You will be shocked to hear that, on reflection, I have become a cautious "Westerner", that is, the war could only be won in the west; though it could not be won there with the existing weapons and tactics.' Liddell Hart did not reply.[19]

Yet Taylor had pulled no punches in his criticism of the Somme campaign of 1916 which, strategically in his opinion, was 'an unredeemed defeat'. The Somme, he added 'set the picture by which future generations saw the First World War: brave helpless soldiers; blundering obstinate generals; nothing achieved. After the Somme men decided that the war would go on for ever'.[20] Two books from the 1960s specifically about the Somme deserve a brief discussion. Brian Gardner's *The Big Push* (1961) was an unambitious popular account relying on mostly familiar published sources. Gardner was sure that a historical verdict would be reached on the battle during the 1960s but hedged his bets as to whether it would be seen as a victory or a disaster. His illustrations and sketch maps clearly suggested the latter, as did his concluding chapter heading 'Napoo!' – soldiers' slang for 'useless', or worse. Anthony Farrar-Hockley's *The Somme* (1964) was much more thoroughly researched, including interviews with survivors, and benefited from the author's first-hand knowledge of the Army's command structure and his distinguished combat experience. He provided excellent coverage of the long gestation of the battle, the first day and 'the long struggle' up to mid-September, but then rather skimped the final stages.[21]

All three books reminded readers that the first day of the battle of the Somme, 1 July 1916, had witnessed one of the worst disasters in British military history, but at this time 'Passchendaele' was still generally taken to be the supreme example of horrific experience on the Western Front for the British Army, as was Verdun for the French. If the first day of the Somme is now popularly used, unhistorically, to characterize the Western Front experience as a whole, this tendency can be traced to Martin Middlebrook's pioneering study in the use of veterans' oral testimony in his *The First Day on the Somme, 1 July 1916*, published in 1971.

Joan Littlewood's Theatre Workshop production *Oh What a Lovely War* (a musical entertainment written by Charles Chilton and members of the cast), was first performed at Stratford East on 19 March 1963. As someone who saw an early performance I can testify that the play was not only highly entertaining but also deeply moving. The puerile sneering at the generals (cribbed from Alan Clark especially) is partly redeemed by oneliners, such as the following.

Master of Whenever there's a crisis, shoot some
 Ceremonies grouse that's what I always say.

Briton I understand he's [President Wilson] a very
 sick man?
American Yes, he's an idealist!

Haig (reading Better conditions needed for officers. The
 from letter) other ranks don't seem to mind so much.[22]

The poignancy was chiefly supplied by the songs, whether savagely satirical ('Forward Joe Soap's Army'), or bitter-sweet and nostalgic ('Chanson de Craonne' and 'They'll Never Believe Us'). But the serious, propaganda message was made clear in the authors' notes, which read more like a political tract than the usual theatre programme.

Thus Raymond Fletcher, the military adviser, described the war as being 'by miscalculation out of accident'. In his view, before 1914 people had believed that the Balance of Power could preserve peace; today 'they believe in the Balance of Terror'. 'But accident and miscalculation are still possible - and a third, nuclear World War could kill as many in four hours as were killed in the whole of World War One.' Another note referred to an American research team which, in planning the Third World War (sic!) in 1960, had deduced from their computers that the 1914–18 war was impossible. There could not have been so many blunders nor so many casualties. Of the play's text it was stated (in italics): *Everything presented as fact is true.*

As a distinguished general and military historian recently remarked,[23] taken as history the play is not even serious enough to be called a travesty, yet from a Marxist viewpoint, Joan Littlewood's production has, allegedly, become dominant in historiography as well as in drama in the cultural understanding of the war. The play's originality lay in presenting the war from the common soldiers' viewpoint: a revolutionary inversion of class precedence in the 1960s, but since then perhaps the dominant mode. A new generation in the 1960s made the shattering discovery – later to be comically trivialized in the BBC television series *Blackadder Goes Forth* (1989) – that 'the Great War represented a betrayal of the ruled by the rulers'.[24] Consequently, once-radical views of the generals' and the staff's incompetence have now become the received wisdom to the extent that to many people it now seems bizarre to insist that there were many able generals and highly efficient staff officers.

The unhistorical nature of the play is evident in its structure. There are only two acts. The first dramatizes innocent hope of victory in a spirit of optimism; the second presents recognition of defeat, in a mood of despair and pessimism. The play leans heavily upon three popular historical texts: Barbara Tuchman's *August 1914* (for the accidental outbreak of war in that year), Alan Clark's *The Donkeys* for 1915, and Leon Wolff's *In Flanders Fields* for 1917. Significantly, from a historian's viewpoint, it has almost nothing to say about 1918, thus avoiding having to explain how 'the donkeys' had secured victory. As early as page 61 of the text a slide depicts a field with white wooden crosses stretching as far as the eye can see: this is what the war was 'about' and how it has ended – in desolation and defeat. Moreover the play deliberately subverted the standard historical accounts of the war as related from the officer's standpoint: instead it gave a voice to a lower class who were supposed only to be able to speak through irony and humour. The line taken was that the war as a whole was visited upon a compliant lower class by an upper class which claimed a superiority it could not justify. To call this approach misleading would be an understatement. These political and cultural concerns, as Derek Paget aptly and damningly concludes, make the play 'a poorish source for knowledge about the Great War, [yet] such an excellent source of knowledge about the early 1960s'.[25]

The play was understandably a great commercial success, and few reviewers seem to have been worried by its blatant anti-military bias or historical distortions. Liddell Hart wrote to the *Observer* that there was more of the real war in the play than in recent 'whitewash history'; it *did* faithfully reflect what his generation thought of the war.[26] Correlli Barnett, however, savaged the production in a BBC Third Programme talk, focusing on the mismatch between entertainment and history. As entertainment it succeeded brilliantly, but in terms of history 'It is a highly partisan, and often grossly unfair, presentation of the war from an extreme anti-Brasshat point of view. Its intent is serious – it wants to make propaganda'.[27]

Richard Attenborough's film adaptation has largely eclipsed the play in the public memory. It caused a sensation world-wide when first screened in 1969, and has been described as 'the perfect TV extravaganza', not least because of its all-star cast. The setting, Brighton Pier, was frivolously satirical, and the dialogue displayed little concern with historical accuracy or fairness. Though obviously 'anti-war', it was more specifically anti-authority and especially anti-officer. The First World War was a disaster because the officer donkeys 'combined homicidal imbecility with vainglorious ambition'. A composite 'Haig figure', representing all the red-tabs, shouldered most of the blame; there were 'butchers' aplenty but 'The Cur' (Lloyd George) was conspicuously absent.[28]

For many viewers the film version excelled the play in its audacious and surrealist final sequence. At the end of the war the surviving soldier of the Smith family is transported to the peace conference and from there follows the red tape out of the room to emerge on the Sussex Downs. There he joins his dead relatives and the family's female survivors. As Jerome Kern's nostalgic melody 'They Wouldn't Believe Me' rises on the sound track the soldiers dissolve into white crosses which are seen to stretch away into infinity filling the whole screen.[29] The effect was overwhelming as an exercise in propaganda but deceitful as history. Curiously, it also did a disservice to the memory of the myriad 'lions' who were made to seem to have thrown away their lives for nothing.

In its supplement previewing the film, the *Observer* had displayed a picture of John Mills in the role of Field Marshal Haig on the cover amid this white sea of crosses and commented 'the hated objects in this film turn out to be a parcel of imbecile aristocrats and politicians, and the British High Command – French and Haig especially'. Its review noted that the film is on the side of the workers who do all the dirty jobs. The superficially glamorous lady, for example, who recruits Harry Smith is seen to be 'a raddled bag as hard as nails', thus suggesting that from the very outset the men have been deceived by their social superiors. The *Sunday Telegraph Review* regarded the film as 'the most pacifist statement since *All Quiet on the Western Front*'. Derek Malcolm in the *Guardian* and Kenneth Allsop in the *Observer* both felt that the film was inferior to the play because its glossy production tended towards a comforting nostalgia and to blandness. As Allsop concluded, 'The raw, caustic savagery which burned through the Theatre Workshop evening still haunts me. I esteem what Mr Attenborough has done, but he hasn't disturbed my nights.'[30] For what it is worth, I agree with those critics who preferred the play for its honest, pacifist attack on 'the establishment', but deplored the film for its dishonest evasions and trivializing of a grand and tragic subject. Between them, the play and the film had transformed a terrible conflict into a light-hearted 'War Game'.

In 1964 Tony Essex produced the biggest documentary series ever made for British television – *The Great War* – in twenty-six parts. The series helped to launch BBC2 and was repeated on BBC1 even while the final episodes were appearing on the new channel. Its appeal was immediate and staggering: the first showing of each episode was watched by an average of eight million viewers.[31]

Although there was an acrimonious controversy about the validity of much that purported to be contemporary front-line film footage, the producer displayed an unusual willingness to adapt visual material to the script, thus in principle giving the writers considerable authority. Chief among the team of well-known historians involved was John Terraine, who wrote the complete script for twelve of the episodes and co-scripted three others.[32] In the previous year Terraine had published *Douglas Haig: the Educated Soldier*, which strongly differed from the contemporary fashion of debunking the generals. But if the high command's viewpoint was thus assured of a fair representation, the series also most positively reflected current concerns to pay homage to the experience of the ordinary soldier or 'everyman at war'. The series – and history subsequently – benefited greatly from a nationwide appeal in 1963 for veterans to describe their personal experiences with the possibility of appearing in the programme.

The *Great War* series made a bold and generally successful attempt to cover all theatres of conflict, air and sea as well as land operations and the political context, particularly on the 'home fronts'. The then director of the Imperial War Museum, Noble Frankland, conducted a determined – but largely unsuccessful – campaign with the producer and the BBC to get the large proportion of reconstructed material used (as distinct from actual battle footage) made clear to the viewers in each episode. Nevertheless it proved to be a breakthrough in the serious deployment of archival material in screened historical subjects.[33]

Unsurprisingly the Western Front episodes proved to be the most controversial. John Terraine, Correlli Barnett and some other members of the script-writing team were determined to counter the prevailing trend of debunking the British Army's performance, and particularly that of its high command and staff, by presenting a more positive, revisionist case.

This led to a clash with the series adviser, B. H. Liddell Hart, who eventually resigned over the Somme episode (number thirteen), and insisted that his name be removed from all lists of credits. In a letter to *The Times* (19 September 1964) explaining his position, Liddell Hart argued that the Somme script was wrongly slanted: it made repeated references to the inexperience and unskilfulness of British troops while not mentioning the indisputable faults of the higher command's planning and conduct of the offensive. He seems to have been particularly troubled by the three reasons attributed to Haig on the first page of the script to justify the offensive: namely that it would relieve pressure on Verdun, assist the Allies in other theatres by preventing the movement of German troops from the Western Front, and would wear down the strength of the forces opposed to the British. Liddell Hart had a valid point that these reasons were afterthoughts drawn from Haig's *Despatches* (1919) and were not those stated at the time. However his protests were largely ignored and the programme went out unchanged to the larger audience on BBC1.[34] Whatever the rights and wrongs of this particular issue, one may suggest that Liddell Hart's meticulous and sometimes pedantic corrections would have made him a difficult collaborator or adviser in any such complicated television production in which time was short and changes costly.

Although the more positive interpretation of Haig's strategy and generalship and the British Army's leading contribution to victory in 1918 were retained in the relevant scripts, the revisionists' hopes were not realized. 'Ironically, the medium proved to be much more powerful than the message. Audience Research Reports revealed that the visual images of the ravaged battlescapes, the broken bodies and the faces of the haggard survivors had made a vastly greater impact than the text. Viewers were struck by the horrors of war and the appalling waste of young men. Thus the series mainly served to confirm the myths which Terraine and some of his colleagues had hoped to demolish or modify; above all the "horror of trench warfare" and the utter futility of the First World War.'[35]

In perspective it is now clear that the *Great War* series played a vital role in introducing the subject seriously to a new generation and in reaching an audience which might not initially have been attracted by scholarly publications. Through its extensive use of film, letters, photographs and the recorded recollections of veterans it gave a powerful boost to the new interest in the ordinary soldiers' experiences, aptly summarized as 'everyman at war'.[36] In due course this stimulus would yield beneficial results, notably in a widespread enthusiasm for visiting the battlefields and close study of particular battles and individual battalions.

These developments were underlined and extended by the excellent part-work publication, Purnell's *History of the First World War*, which appeared in 128 weekly parts between 1969 and 1971. The series was edited first by Barrie Pitt and later by Brigadier Peter Young, with Liddell Hart as editor-in-chief. With authoritative contributors, lavish illustrations and suggestions for further reading, these concise articles formed ideal introductions to almost every conceivable aspect of the First World War. Thirty years later, many are still worth reading, so much so indeed that they constitute tempting 'cribs' for hard-pressed undergraduates with essay deadlines.

Through the 1960s and 1970s, when the ultra-critical views of the Western Front strategy and British generalship, as disseminated by *Oh What a Lovely War*, gained a powerful hold on public opinion, John Terraine waged a stubborn attritional counter-bombardment. Critics might sneer at 'Tommy Terraine' (and some did), suggesting that the ten books he published on the war between *Mons* (1960) and *White Heat: the New Warfare* (1982) were repetitive, blinkered and obsessive. But already, by 1991, it was becoming clear that he had made a significant contribution to popular conceptions of the war,[37] and since then, as I shall argue in my final chapter, his position in 'the trenches' has been considerably reinforced.

Terraine's most important book, *Douglas Haig: the Educated Soldier*, was published in 1963. While presenting the best possible case for its subject, it was far from uncritical and certainly not deserving of the dismissive pun 'Haigiography'. Several leading military historians of the day, including A. J. P. Taylor, to Liddell Hart's chagrin, reviewed the book favourably. Taylor's just criticism was that Terraine had been fair to Haig but not to Lloyd George: 'He [Haig] did as well as any other British general could have done, and probably better. When men look back to the carnage of the time, they feel that this was not enough.' Michael Howard in the *Sunday Times* contrasted Terraine's study with the recent 'pullulation of worthless books on the First World War' which had abused Haig's reputation. He interestingly linked Haig's style of generalship and strategy with that of Moltke and Grant, both highly successful commanders in nineteenth-century wars. Alistair Horne also noticed the book favourably in the *Sunday Telegraph*.[38]

In book after book (and in numerous articles) Terraine reiterated his main points. The First World War was not unique and *sui generis*, as Paul Fussell and others have asserted or assumed: it should be viewed rather in the wider context of industrial mass warfare, including the American Civil War and the Second World War. But material conditions in the First World War ruled out brilliant generalship or any quick route to victory for two main reasons: commanders were deprived of the direct voice control of their predecessors and of the wireless communications of their successors; and poor tactical means of mobility entailed that the defensive would hold an advantage over the offensive. Next, he pointed out that from mid-1916 until the end of the war Britain, uniquely in its history, bore the main burden of the war on the crucial front and against a very powerful enemy. Attrition warfare and heavy casualties were unavoidable: British generals were no worse, indeed perhaps better, than those of the other belligerents. Finally, the war had to be won on land, above all on the Western Front, and *was* won by the Allies, with Haig and his armies playing the leading role.

Terraine had his limitations and blind spots, and it would not be surprising if at times he was driven into dogmatic or more extreme positions in fending off his critics. As Taylor's review of *Haig* indicated, in championing the generals (or 'Brasshats') he is markedly unsympathetic to the 'Frockcoats', notably Lloyd George. As regards sources, he tended to stick with the official histories, biographies and other published works which were available in the 1960s, and did not much avail himself of the archival collections which were opened from the end of the decade. Perhaps most seriously, there is a pronounced note of determinism in his approach which is most obviously evident in the subtitle of his book on Passchendaele: 'A Study in

Inevitability'. As one thoughtful critic has pointed out, by stressing the great extent to which external factors (weaponry, transport, communications) constricted innovation in tactics and strategy, Terraine makes it very difficult for himself to allow for innovations and improvements. Furthermore, his thesis, 'despite its deep understanding of modern industrial warfare, leads the reader away from a perfectly natural British desire to criticise the conduct of the war that cost so many lives, to the rather Panglossian conclusion that the Great War was, in fact the *best of all possible wars*'.[39]

Be that as it may, thanks to Terraine and other historians we can now understand, if we wish to, that commanders had very limited room to manoeuvre – in every sense. Moreover, despite all the errors and shortcomings, it is possible to reach the conclusion that Britain's war effort, on both the home and military 'fronts', was very impressive indeed.

These views are still controversial and had certainly not gained wide acceptance by the end of the 1960s; indeed, they remained unpopular if not incomprehensible. As Alex Danchev suggested in concluding his scintillating analysis of 'bunking' and debunking in the 1960s, the overall effect of the upsurge of renewed interest in the Great War was to revive and perpetuate the impression made on the public by the anti-war memoirs of the late 1920s and early 1930s. In the play and the film of *Oh What A Lovely War* 'The generational ghosts were rattling their chains in the 1960s – once more – through the incantatory names of the villages and rivers and battlefields, the numbers of dead and the dates now flashing a garish reminder on the screen . . . ("October 12 1917, Passchendaele – British loss in three hours 13,000 men – gain 100 yards"). The enormity of the event was the ruling concern.'[40] Are the generational ghosts still rattling their chains, and does the compelling myth resurrected in the 1960s still prevail? This will be the subject of my final chapter.

4 **Thinking the unthinkable**
the First World War as history

Ten years ago, in an editorial introduction to a collection of essays *The First World War and British Military History* (1991), I suggested that 'The time is surely approaching, if it has not already arrived, when the First World War can be studied simply as history without polemic intent or apologies'. This hope and expectation has not been realized; indeed, the gulf between serious historical studies and popular misconceptions, encouraged by the media, may even be widening. This is a somewhat depressing state of affairs which historians must do their best to remedy. Public interest in the First World War has recently become more intense, due mainly to the development of a battlefield tourist industry, so there is certainly an audience and readership to be reached.

In this chapter I shall first explore a small sample of the works which perpetuate myths, stereotypes and caricatures about the British role on the Western Front, before concluding with a survey of some of the positive developments which provide reasons for guarded optimism about the future understanding of this very important subject.

In recent years there have been mercifully few polemical works like John Laffin's *British Butchers and Bunglers of World War One* (1988)[1] or Denis Winter's *Haig's Command* (1991),[2] which essentially reworked the old 'lions led by donkeys' theme of the 1960s with, at best, the substitution of 'weasels' for 'donkeys'.[3] Military publishers are generally aware that more scholarly, though still critical, research is now widely available.

On the literary front, Paul Fussell's *The Great War and Modern Memory* (1975), although savagely reviewed by respected military historians,[4] still continues to exert powerful influence, not least in its post-modernist argument that the Western Front can only be understood as a unique, unhistorical event taking place outside time. By popularizing an approach to the war through literature and cultural artefacts Fussell has contributed greatly to what one scholar has termed the emergence of 'Two Western Fronts'.[5]

Two fictional bestsellers of the 1990s display the tendency to dwell on 'the horrors' of the Western Front. In *Birdsong* (1993) Sebastian Faulks made full use of soldiers' diaries and letters to recreate in imaginative terms an extreme view of the slaughter on the Somme on 1 July 1916 and of the worst nightmares of the tunnellers' war which was more applicable to the Ypres sector in 1917. Pat Barker's trilogy, *Regeneration* (1991), *The Eye in the Door* (1993) and *The Ghost Road* (1995), essentially recreated for a modern readership the story of the breakdowns of the war poets Sassoon and Owen and their treatment by the psychologist W. H. Rivers at Craiglockhart Hospital in Edinburgh. But she introduced a cynical, lower class, bisexual officer, Billy Prior, to provide a late twentieth-century interest, notably in this character's loathing of the war and sordid sexual exploits which leave nothing to the imagination.[6] The story's culmination in *The Ghost Road* is reminiscent of *All Quiet on the Western Front* in the deaths in combat of the main characters, Wilfred Owen (in actuality) and Billy Prior and his comrades in fiction. In a final harrowing scene, Lieutenant Hallet, ex-public schoolboy, son of a regular officer and former believer in the justice of the war, is dying in Rivers's hospital ward with half his face shot away. In his death agony he cries out repeatedly 'shotvarfet', which Rivers translates as 'It's not worth it'. All the wounded soldiers in the ward echo the cry and even Rivers feels impelled to join in. This is the authentic whingeing note of the 1990s transposed unconvincingly to 1918. As Stephen Badsey has recently written:

> It is doubtful if any British play, film or television dramatisation of the Western Front since perhaps 1950 has depicted something that was actually a commonplace of the war: a competent officer bravely and successfully leading his troops.[7]

In 1998 Professor Hugh Brogan criticized David Haig's play *My Boy Jack* (about Rudyard Kipling's son, John, killed in the battle of Loos) and its reviewers for the general assumption that the war was pointless, and that the dead died uselessly. To a historian, he wrote, 'the piece was a travesty of the past and a confirmation . . . that the myth has displaced truth'. It is, he added, 'a generation that has succumbed to sentimentality and "presentism", that is, inability to grasp that different values prevailed in the past'.[8]

William Boyd's first venture into film directing in 1999, *The Trench*, focused in minute detail on an infantry platoon in the forty-eight hours before the start of the battle of the Somme on 1 July 1916 which was, to put it mildly, unoriginal.[9] It was difficult to avoid stereotypes in portraying the main characters, and there were echoes of other plays, films and novels. In 1998 *Oh What a Lovely War* was revived and toured ten provincial locations under a custom-built big top. In an interview the thirty-three year-old director, Fiona Laird, suggested that the drama would have to be more radical to shock a new cynical generation more used to satirizing and cocking a snook at people in authority than that of the sixties.[10] In the same year an Imperial War Museum exhibition of the cultural legacy of the war was reviewed by a novelist, Adam Thorpe, who employed familiar words such as 'horror', 'nightmare', 'futility', and 'utter barbarism'. He noted that Wilfred Owen, according to a recent survey, remained the nation's favourite modern poet: 'Schoolchildren still hear Owen's shrill, demented shells before (or more likely in place of) the innumerable bees of Tennyson.' He added that Britten's *War Requiem* included Owen's poems in its libretto and that a CD recording of the work has a picture of trenches on its cover.[11]

Most recently (in 1999) BBC drama portrayed the Gallipoli campaign in *All the King's Men*. In a far-fetched and quite unnecessary misrepresentation of the historical record, David Jason played the elderly but naive commander of the Sandringham estate's Territorial Army battalion whose faith in the competence of his superiors leads to the pointless annihilation of his men.[12]

The eightieth anniversary of the battle of the Somme in 1996 prompted two significant television programmes. On 3 July *Timewatch* presented a portrait of *Douglas Haig: the Unknown Soldier* whose producer, Helen Bettinson, made a most commendable attempt to achieve fairness and balance, so much so indeed that some of my comments would be more appropriately placed in the positive part of this balance sheet. On the critical side, however, the offensive was led by an almost apoplectic John Laffin who made all the usual charges: Haig was a cavalryman obsessed with horses to the exclusion of technical innovation; he was a chateau general completely out of touch with the front; his reliance on God was blasphemous, and he was as stubborn as a donkey. Laffin repeatedly charged Haig with criminal negligence. His most unpleasant comment was that the public would have cheered any commander-in-chief in 1918, even Charlie Chaplin. Gerard de Groot and Keith Simpson criticized some aspects of Haig's methods of command, such as his over-optimism about enemy casualties, and his persistence in the Third Ypres campaign, but from an informed standpoint. Other negative aspects included an opening sequence from 'Blackadder' to set up the accepted stereotype, an undue emphasis on *British* casualties and a mournful commentary by Kirsty Wark. The pro-Haig case was well put by Trevor Wilson (an Australasian to counter Laffin) who, *inter alia*, pointed out Lloyd George's failings as prime minister, and by Gary Sheffield and John Hussey. Sheffield, in particular, provoked some angry responses by stating that the Somme campaign was a turning point in the British Army's 'learning curve' and that by 1917 it was already very effective. He was also filmed in a war cemetery at Passchendaele telling officer cadets that Haig deserved to be taken seriously as a military commander.

The programme was watched by more than three and a half million people. Although it opened a door to a balanced judgement on Haig, particularly in terms of television, press coverage without exception showed how wide the gulf still is between historians and intelligent reviewers.[13] It is scarcely credible, but four of the critics took the *Blackadder* series as the historical truth against which to evaluate the programme. *The Times* reviewer, for example, was frankly puzzled by the programme and admitted his near-total ignorance of Haig and military tactics. Stuart Jeffries stated that 420,000 British soldiers were *killed* on the Somme – a huge inflation. Sean Day-Lewis, one of the reviewers who judged Haig on the basis of *Blackadder*, utterly rejected the revisionist arguments, concluding facetiously that Haig's 'wisest move was to become a semi-retired donkey, let his lions lead the way and save his energy for the consequent victory parades'. Roy Hattersley, also writing in *The Times*, similarly rejected all the points made in defence or mitigation, commenting snidely on Haig's famous order of the day at the crisis of the German Spring Offensive in 1918, that he 'fought with his back against the wall of a chateau 40 miles from the front line'. Other reports, including those in the *Observer*, the *Daily Telegraph*, and the *Independent* revealed considerable ignorance about important events in the war, and seemed (in Nigel Cave's words) to be metaphorically 'strung up on their own impenetrable barbed wire mental stronghold that it was the British Army that uniquely bled in the war'. The depressing conclusion must be that the producer's daring but by no means extravagant attempt to open up new perspectives on the frequently condemned but little understood historical figure was seriously distorted by the ignorance and prejudices of the leading press reviewers. Their verdict was that if distinguished historians from Britain, Australia and the United States believed that Haig had been misunderstood and criticized excessively then their opinions must be rejected, because *Blackadder* encapsulated the essential truths about Haig and the Western Front.

By contrast, the seven-part television series *1914–1918: the Great War and the Shaping of the 20th Century*, presented by the American team of Jay Winter and Blaine Baggett in December 1996, was not revisionist but rather tended to reinforce traditional views. Seductive, and at times bewitching, photography may have entertained its large audience, but this was an unsatisfactory mixture of social and military history, concentrating on the cultural impact of the war as it was 'endured by millions of ordinary men and women'. In the British episodes particularly the pervasive tone of gloom and despondency was underlined by the keening commentary spoken by Judi Dench 'in a schoolmistressy style and at a slow march in time to funereal music'. Footage was plundered from various phases of the war and shown out of chronological order.[14]

The most scathing critique appeared in the *Spectator* on 18 January 1997 under the title 'Oh What a Whingeing War'. Correlli Barnett, a principal scriptwriter for the 1964 BBC series *The Great War*, justifiably felt that this later version was greatly inferior to the original. Barnett's main criticisms concerned the inadequate or non-existent coverage of theatres of the war other than the Western Front, and the poor presentation which relied too heavily on 'talking heads', speaking in the 'historic present tense'. Indeed the 'series historian', Jay Winter, irritated Barnett so much that he longed to punch him! Barnett deplored the emphasis on casualties, grief and hardship at the expense of patriotic enthusiasm, belief in the cause and popular resilience and humour. The guiding spirits seemed to be those of Wilfred Owen and 'the brave but whingeing poet', Siegfried Sassoon. The final episodes harp on the lost generation rather than the significance of the Allied victory, and the concluding scenes return to Sassoon at his gloomiest, to disturbing footage of shellshock cases, war graves and spiritualist attempts to get in touch with dead soldiers.

While it would be unduly harsh to say that these cultural concerns are irrelevant, Barnett is surely right to lament the omission of the most crucial aspect; namely an attempt to explain the political and strategic dynamics of the war 'which alone can give meaning to the human experiences so glumly harped on here'. This seems to me to be the main defect in nearly all literary and cultural interpretations of the war. If policy and strategy are omitted, or not properly explained, then terms like 'pointless' and 'futile' all too easily slip in as a natural response to the destruction and heavy casualties. Barnett's final lament was that this series was produced by the BBC Education Department and that this 'politically correct telly tract will be fed to our young in schools and universities as "history"'.

Perhaps the most revealing insight into public and, more especially, political views of the First World War in the later 1990s was the prolonged and well-organized campaign, in 1997–8, to grant a posthumous blanket pardon to the 306 British soldiers executed for crimes in the war zone other than those which would have drawn the death penalty in a civil court. Although the campaign, led by the Labour MP Andrew Mackinlay, with support from the Royal British Legion, focused on soldiers executed for cowardice and desertion, other military crimes were included, such as sleeping on sentry duty and 'casting away a weapon in the face of the enemy'. The basic facts were that some 20,000 soldiers were found guilty of military crimes for which the death penalty could have been passed. Just over 3,000 were actually sentenced to death but more than 90 per cent had their sentences commuted by their commanders-in-chief.[15] The records of those executed were preserved, whereas for the vast majority not executed they were destroyed. British military justice is often compared unfavourably with that in the German army, but it was less severe, in the numbers of soldiers executed, than either France or Italy. Undoubtedly there were some 'hard cases' or cases of dubious justice among those executed. On the other hand British discipline and morale held firm throughout the war and the number executed was miniscule compared with the millions who served and did their duty.

After a very thorough parliamentary review, the issue was debated in the House of Commons on 24 July 1998. The Minister for the Armed Forces, John Reid, declared that 'we cannot and do not condone cowardice, desertion, mutiny or assisting the enemy' – although that is what some campaigners did seem to propose. Reid was obliged to admit that the review had confirmed that the procedures for courts martial were correct, given the law as it stood at that time. The grounds for a blanket legal pardon on the basis of unsafe conviction simply did not exist. A review of individual cases would leave the vast majority still condemned or re-condemned, thus bringing further anguish to the families concerned. While the formality of pardon was therefore impossible, Reid felt that the enquiry had cast great doubt on the stigma of condemnation. He expressed the remarkable view that 'In a sense those who were executed were as much victims of the war' as those killed in action; in short they were 'the victims with millions of others, of a cataclysmic and ghastly war'. He repeated the phrase about all being 'victims' in urging that those responsible in local authorities should consider adding the missing names to books of remembrance and war memorials throughout the land.

In responding to Keith Simpson's Opposition statement that it was much better to leave history alone, Reid replied that 'The conditions and nature of the First World War distinguished it from all others'. Mackinlay added the puzzling remark that these ordinary British soldiers and other victims were themselves 'the victims of the decisions of selfish people'. To whom was he referring? Presumably to the junior and middle-rank officers who were ordered to take part in courts martial, and to senior officers whose responsibility it was to maintain discipline with a view to winning the war. Subsequent speakers nearly all evinced strong endorsement of Mackinlay's viewpoint, regretting that a blanket pardon had not been possible. Only Edward Garnier delicately touched on a point familiar to military historians in asking the minister 'to bear in mind what others at the time may have thought, rather than what we think now at this distance'.

The minister's statement and the ensuing parliamentary debate have by no means ended the campaign for a blanket pardon for those executed. In spring 2000 the

Ypres Museum of the First World War organized a seminar on 'Unquiet graves' at which the pro-pardon lobby was strongly represented. The chairperson's introduction reminded delegates that the armies of 1914–18 were 'led to the slaughter like so many great herds . . . with fear alone keeping them in line: fear of the blindfold; fear of the execution squad; and fear of death at dawn'. This was re-writing history with a vengeance but, as John Hughes-Wilson reported, European collective memories of the war differ greatly and for some delegates history was evidently not a matter of fact but 'an agenda to be exploited'. A member of the Scottish Parliament voiced the unpatriotic opinion that Haig should have been shot too! When historians pointed out that all armed forces needed discipline and that an important purpose of military law was to ensure that the commander's will was enforced 'a shocked murmur rippled through the hall'. As Colonel Hughes-Wilson concluded, such emotional, anti-war manifestations which show no respect for history will not help those select cases where there is a case for judicial review.[16]

The eightieth anniversary of the Armistice in November 1998 provided a focus for anti-First World War effusions by non-historians and by 'historians' who did not deserve that title. The *Daily Express* led the way with the front-page headline on 6 November: 'Why do we let this man cast a shadow over our war dead?' accompanied by a photograph of Haig's equestrian statue in Whitehall and a proposal that the statue be melted down and the metal used to mint medals for families of those executed as deserters and mutineers. The editorial, claiming that its views represented 'the modern generation of military historians,'[17] stated that Earl Haig 'bears a heavy and perhaps unforgivable responsibility for those deaths' (i.e., hundreds of thousands who died needlessly), and it repeated the jibe that 'British soldiers endured a miserable existence in the rat-infested trenches while Field Marshal Haig and his staff lived a life of luxury in a chateau far behind the lines'. The late Alan Clark weighed in with an article full of factual errors and tendentious remarks of which any serious historian would be ashamed. His main thesis, often repeated, was that Britain had made a fatal error in entering an avoidable war and then been ruined by criminally inept strategy and tactics. Only the poets, particularly Wilfred Owen, writing 'on scraps of paper in ill-lit dug-outs' had revealed the full horror of events. 'A complete future generation ... just ceased to exist.' Most people now realize, he claimed, that it was Haig who 'threw it all away'.

The newspaper's campaign to have Haig's statue demolished was stillborn, but the statue continues to provide a focus for anti-military expression. More recently, when anti-capitalist demonstrators daubed statues with paint, the writer A. N. Wilson was moved to comment, under the headline 'Statues they should have vandalised': 'Down Whitehall a few yards, Field Marshal Haig, arguably a mass murderer whose only redeeming quality was incompetence [sic], should, perhaps, never have been honoured by a statue in the first instance'.[18]

Returning to November 1998, Allan Massie, a distinguished man of letters but not a historian, repeated in the *Spectator* (7 November 1998) the Alan Clark indictment that by entering the First World War Britain had ensured the stalemate on the Western Front, and in doing so, 'prolonged the most terrible war Europe had yet seen'. The consequences were easily summarized: Soviet Russia, Fascist Italy, Nazi Germany, the war of 1939–45. In an error-packed paragraph which even got Haig's first name wrong, Max Hastings reinforced the myth of a high command living a life of luxury while presiding for four years over the greatest of military disasters. Like most of his fellow generals Sir John Haig [sic] 'dined nightly off china and crystal among the finest fare that Montreuil could provide'.[19]

Finally there is the phenomenon of Blackadder, truly the representative popular image of the Western Front for the 1990s. As we noted in the previous chapter,[20] the once radical discovery that the First World War had witnessed a betrayal of the ruled by the rulers 'had given way to the comically deconstructive *Blackadder Goes Forth*' (BBC television, 1989). The current received wisdom depicts Haig and his fellow generals as Melchett-like figures of incompetence and callousness.

Should this highly successful television series, released on video and audio cassette, be taken seriously by cultural and military historians? *Blackadder Goes Forth*, although primarily a comedy with echoes in the folk memory of *1066 and All That*, also has dark undertones and a poignant finale as the leading characters go 'over the top' and into oblivion. It encapsulates the popular myth of the First World War as an unmitigated disaster. Gary Sheffield began his survey in *War, Culture and the Media* in 1996 with a discussion of Blackadder, and more recently Stephen Badsey has developed his themes, treating *Blackadder Goes Forth* as the key text in what he terms the 'Two Western Fronts' debate. As early as 1994, at an international conference at Leeds, the *Blackadder* series was cited as serving to 'perpetuate myths which persist in the face of strong contrary evidence'. As already mentioned, it was employed as an introduction and touchstone for the television programme on Haig in 1996 and, the ultimate accolade, in 2000 it was popularly voted number nine in *100 Great Television Moments* for the most memorable television events of the century (only one other fictional episode made it into the top ten). Some schools are now using *Blackadder Goes Forth* as the main text for study of the First World War at General Certificate of Secondary Education (GCSE) level.[21]

Perhaps a little unfairly, *Blackadder* has been called *'Journey's End* with jokes'. Badsey explores the close similarities and also the contrasts between the two and concludes that by the late 1980s Sherriff's portrayal of the behaviour and attitudes of officers and men in the trenches had become so remote from popular understanding that it had to be superseded for a mass audience as the farce of *Blackadder*, which would still embody key myths about the British role on the Western Front. Thus, as Badsey concludes, *Blackadder* has provided a focal point for the debate regarding 'the Western Front of literature and popular culture against the Western Front of history'.

Ian Beckett and Gary Sheffield have both recently written critically of the way in which the First World War is taught in British schools, the former remarking that the GCSE syllabus tends 'to reinforce stereotypes of the Western Front as a theatre of unrelieved terror, deprivation and disillusionment lacking all meaning', while the latter gained the impression that very little revisionist history had yet filtered into recommended school text books.[22] Stage Three of the National Curriculum requires the First World War to be studied in outline by every fourteen-year-old pupil, while the Western Front is an option which can be studied in greater depth, but seldom is, at senior level in schools.[23] The GCSE National Curriculum provides a sound overall coverage of the war in note form and suggests a variety of sensible, searching and reasonably objective questions while leaving a great deal of flexibility to the individual teacher. As a current debate in the Western Front Association *Bulletin* shows,[24] some teachers who are keen students of military history try to provide up-to-date publications and take their classes on academically challenging battlefield tours. But many more lack this personal interest and have little time to devote to the war in a packed syllabus. Also on the negative side, I have been invited, over the past few years, to address sixth form conferences on the First World War in Chester, Salford and Leicester, but all had to be cancelled due to lack of interest.

It seems likely that teachers of English rather than history still have more influence in the shaping of views on the First World War, through the teaching of war poetry, and from a narrow selection of poems, especially those of Owen and Sassoon. Special coach tours are organized to the battlefields for children studying the 'war poets', and an annual conference is held at the Imperial War Museum on this subject. Christopher Somerville, who went on a war poets tour as an adult in 1999, recalled that at eighteen years old, reading 'The Show' and other illusion-shattering poems by Wilfred Owen, his eyes were opened to horror and sadness: 'the notes those writers struck still resonate today, drawing pilgrims in their thousands to Picardy and Flanders'.[25] This concentration on a literary view of the war is not necessarily objectionable in itself, but the selection of poems and concentration of the tours on the cemeteries does tend to reinforce the assumption of the pointless waste of young lives.

Also perturbing is a recent issue of *Teaching History*, published by the *Historical Association* specially for school teachers. The cover of the May 1999 issue portrays a sergeant glumly surveying a montage of poppies blazoned with the lines:

> Man by man the regiment falls,
> like a tidal wave falling and slowing,
> And slowing and falling.

It emerges that these lines were part of a poem composed by a schoolboy, Matthew, as part of a project for eleven to eighteen year-olds at a comprehensive school to 'motivate pupils through poetic writing about the First World War'. The methodology is explained, stage by stage, and it must be said that some of the resulting poems are impressive. The final question posed, however, is 'they loved doing it, but was it history?', to which a positive answer is given. The children will try to avoid anachronism, and will remember and understand. 'Knowing in their hearts and remembering vividly the horror of trench warfare, they will understand Chamberlain's desire for appeasement. They will be able to develop as historians.'[26] One wonders why Hitler's direct and prolonged personal experience of the horrors of trench warfare did not incline him towards appeasement.

Let us now consider some positive and encouraging developments which should contribute to a wider understanding of the First World War as history. One significant social phenomenon has been a rivival, since the later 1980s, of public interest in the nationwide commemoration of Armistice Day which reflected a widespread upsurge of interest in the First World War. After a period in the mid-1980s when white poppies were again sold in competition with red ones, which were held by pacifists to glorify war, the Royal British Legion and its supporters campaigned vigorously to have the national two minutes' silence restored on 11 November as distinct from the nearest Sunday. The breakthrough was achieved in 1995 when a substantial proportion of the nation observed the silence on 11 November, and by the time of the eightieth anniversary in 1998 supermarkets, banks, and road, rail and air transport had all welcomed the pause – or at least conformed – to make this an extremely moving occasion. There are still criticisms from the left to the effect that 'nationalist politicians and militarists' milk the occasion for all it is politically worth, whether that means gaining a few votes or avoiding responsibility for their role in the killing; whereas on the right the rush of certain MPs to display plastic poppies many days in advance was viewed as 'self-serving humbug', and proof that the once painful memories were losing their hold on the nation. Despite these contrasting views, however, the public respect for all the ceremonies connected with Armistice Day now seems stronger than at any time in the latter half of the twentieth century.[27]

The revival of popular interest in the First World War is nowhere better illustrated than in the development of the Western Front Association. Founded in 1980 by the author John Giles, with John Terraine as its first long-term president and chief inspiration, the WFA has proved to be a very successful association. It is noteworthy that only a few of its members had served in the First World War; most joined for a variety of scholarly, family and leisure interests. Its stated aim is 'to further the interest in the period 1914–1918', and its principal objective is to 'perpetuate the memory, courage and comradeship of those, on all sides, who served their country in France and Flanders'. It does not seek to justify or glorify war and is entirely nonpolitical. Some twenty years after its foundation the WFA continues to flourish. It now has forty-one branches in the United Kingdom and eleven overseas and affiliated associations. Total British membership has grown from 282 in 1980 to 3,500 in 1990, and 5,000 today.[28] All the branches stage lecture programmes, battlefield tours and other social activities. An annual summer conference open to all members is held in Wales. The WFA publishes an excellent magazine *Stand To!* and an in-house general news *Bulletin*. Although many members have specific interests or hobbies related to the Western Front which are not strictly scholarly, nevertheless the value of amateur research and publications should not be underestimated, because the latter provide many invaluable building blocks from which grander edifices may be constructed.

Professor Richard Holmes's deservedly popular television presentation of successive series of *War Walks* and more recently *The Western Front* may be put in the credit balance in view of the author's lightly worn knowledge, empathy with the soldiers' experience and rare ability to communicate his enthusiasm on camera. These programmes must have persuaded thousands of viewers to visit the battlefields and to become active students of the First World War.

Perhaps under editorial direction, however, the six-part *Western Front* series adhered closely to the 'doom and gloom' traditional approach, which gave little scope for any modification to accommodate recent revisionist research. For example, no one would have gathered from the unrelenting, grim depiction of the Third Ypres campaign that there was a hot and dry spell in September and early October during which Plumer's Second Army demonstrated its tactical superiority. The series as a whole concentrated on Allied defeats and disasters such as Verdun and the Somme, allowing only seven minutes out of three hours for the allies' victorious advance between July and November 1918. The BBC book of the series differs markedly from the television script and, in scholarly terms, is far superior.[29] The book is organized thematically, from 'Making the Front' to 'Breaking the Front', with a sensitive text that displays up-to-date knowledge and a judicious handling of controversial issues. While stressing the high casualty figures and the various dreadful ways in which soldiers might die, Holmes also endorses John Terraine's argument, that for the only time in its history Britain bore the brunt of the fighting in the principal theatre against a first-rate enemy's main strength. The implication is that there was no obvious alternative to attrition and heavy losses. On the final advance he quotes Foch's tribute: 'Never at any time in history has the British army achieved greater results in attack than in this unbroken offensive.' It is a pity that many more viewers will have watched the series on television than will buy and carefully read the book.

Over the past twenty years or so the First World War has at last received the attention of a wide range of scholars who have begun to exploit the vast documentary sources now available. Although these historians differ on some points they are all concerned to debate the issues seriously with a view to advancing knowledge and understanding. In time, it must be hoped, this body of impressive work – published or in progress – will dispel some of the ignorance and combat the myths discussed in this book.

Here, first, are just a few of the key publications which provide the starting point for contemporary students of the war: Shelford Bidwell and Dominick Graham, *Firepower* (1982); Trevor Wilson, *The Myriad Faces of War* (1986); Tim Travers, *The Killing Ground* (1987); David French *British Strategy and War Aims, 1914–1916* (1986) and *The Strategy of the Lloyd George Coalition, 1916–1918* (1985); John Bourne, *Britain and the Great War* (1989); Paddy Griffith, *Battle Tactics of the Western Front* (1992); and an excellent survey of current international scholarship on the war, Hugh Cecil and Peter Liddle (eds.), *Facing Armageddon: The First World War Experienced* (1996). Since these lectures were given, and revised for publication, several excellent new books have appeared, including Ian Beckett's *The Great War, 1914–1918* (2001) and Gary Sheffield's *Forgotten Victory. The First World War: Myths and Realities* (2001). These authors and other scholars actively engaged in research, including Peter Simkins, Stephen Badsey, John Lee, Hew Strachan and Nigel Cave should, collectively, banish forever such backward-looking polemical titles as 'The Donkeys' and 'British Butchers and Bunglers of World War One'.

Before examining the critical question of the British Expeditionary Force's learning experience on the Western Front I want, briefly, to outline some other new approaches which offer fresh perspectives on the war and, by doing so, reveal the magnitude of our ignorance in the recent past.

First, what might be termed the 'Péronne School', from its research and conference centre or *historial* there, under the inspiration of the Cambridge scholar Jay Winter, has, since the early 1990s, published a stream of pioneering studies on social and cultural aspects of the war. Winter himself has produced important work on casualties and demography, while other scholars have studied topics such as the ceremonial remembrance of the war, war memorials (a very popular new research area) and war damage.[30] While this study centre consciously departs from more traditional concerns with generalship, strategy and tactics, its publications and conferences all serve to encourage the serious study of the war from a comparative standpoint covering all the belligerent nations.

Although there are still some significant gaps to be filled, we now know a great deal more than we did twenty years ago about the unprecedented achievement of the British 'nation in arms' with its constituent elements of regulars, territorials, volunteers and conscripts. Peter Simkins covered the raising and training of the Kitchener Armies in exemplary fashion and we eagerly await the complementary study of 'the Haig Armies'.[31] The same author has charted the development since the late 1960s of what he aptly terms 'everyman at war'. The Imperial War Museum and the Liddle Collection at Leeds University, in particular, house vast treasure troves of diaries, letters and other memorabilia relating to every conceivable aspect of soldiers' experiences in the war, and these sources have been supplemented by recorded interviews with veterans – a special feature of the publications of Martin Middlebrook, Lyn Macdonald and Malcolm Brown. As mentioned earlier, Middlebrook's trail-blazing study *The First Day on the Somme* inspired a number of books of varied quality on the 'Pals battalions' and their fateful debut on the Western Front. This has had the unfortunate effect of creating an obsessive media interest in the BEF's worst day of the whole war, thereby fortifying the myth of incompetence and pointless slaughter which is all too often applied to the whole Somme campaign, and indeed to Western Front operations throughout.[32]

Another important topic now receiving scholarly attention is morale and discipline. It is already ten years since John Fuller published *Troop Morale and Popular Culture in the British and Dominion Armies, 1914–1918*[33] which argued that the availability of mass popular culture in the rear areas was an essential factor in maintaining British morale. More recently, by contrast, Gary Sheffield's book *Leadership in the Trenches* has placed the main emphasis on the practical effectiveness of officer–other ranks relations and the acceptable paternalism of the British officer corps.[34]

The ability to name say, a dozen senior British commanders on the Western Front might be a criterion for serious acquaintance with the subject. The television programme on Sir Douglas Haig, discussed earlier, was subtitled 'The Unknown Soldier' and, although in his case *'the only known soldier'* might have been more accurate, it is true that even his army commanders are unknown to the general public.[35] John Bourne is currently studying the 1,234 officers who attained the rank of brigadier-general and above in Western Front commands.[36] His research stresses the rapid increase in the number of generals from a basis of extremely limited experience in 1914 (only three officers had commanded a corps even in peacetime), and the rapid turnover (30 per cent 'casualties' for various reasons in the first year of war alone). The great majority who eventually became generals had been regular officers pre-1914 – a sign of conservatism – but on the other hand

many dominions commanders were quite experienced and
'professional', not the superior gifted amateurs beloved of
critics such as Liddell Hart. In character and qualities the
generals were as varied as one would expect in other profes-
sions, but most owed their opportunity to intensive talent-
spotting and selection. Qualities sought for included independence of mind, robustness in health and temperament,
proven experience in command and, above all, aggression.
Some otherwise competent generals were relieved or dis-
missed for showing insufficient aggression, while a few others such as Haking and Hunter-Weston may have survived,
despite other failings, simply because they *were* aggressive. One popular misconception, at least, will be dispelled
by Bourne's research: there were, despite Plumer's decep-
tive appearance, no elderly Crimean-style commanders on
the Western Front – at least by 1916. The average age of
major-generals (division commanders) fell during the war
from fifty-seven to just under forty-seven. 'Boy' Bradford
commanded a brigade at twenty-five and H. K. Bethell a
division (66th) at thirty-five. Even allowing for these exceptionally young appointees, the average compares well with
divisional commanders in the Second World War. While
the selection process remains somewhat mysterious and
some regrettable errors were made, either in promoting officers above their ability or in sacking other competent ones
as scapegoats, the overriding concern, from Haig down-
wards, was to secure the best commanders at every level to
win the war.

Another myth which should be dispelled by recent research is that senior officers, safe in their chateaux far behind the lines, were immune from the casualties that their
orders inflicted on the lower ranks. In fact 232 officers of
general rank were wounded, of whom 78 were killed in
action, or died of wounds or as a result of active service. The
majority of those killed in action were the victims of shells

or small arms fire. Ten of them held the Victoria Cross and 126 the Distinguished Service Order, several with bar. These figures contrast sharply with those of the Second World War where only about twenty general officers were killed or died of wounds.[37]

Closely related to the evaluation of commanders, there is also important research in progress on the comparative performance of divisions, particularly in relation to the highly charged question of the relative merits of British and dominion formations. Peter Simkins and Gary Sheffield have argued persuasively that although the dominion divisions had certain obvious advantages in the physical quality of their men (mostly volunteers, although Canada eventually introduced conscription), and more coherent and permanent organization, by 1918 there was no great gulf between them and the elite British divisions. Indeed, the evidence suggests that in the final operations of 'the hundred days', even ordinary British divisions such as the 30th and 46th were of a high overall quality, in contrast to the German army, where elite formations were raised at the expense of the remainder. An ambitious project is also in hand to compile a database for all British divisions on the Western Front, which should eventually enable those interested to assess comparative performance on more objective criteria.[38]

Our understanding of the quality of generalship and the performance of units and formations will be seriously flawed without systematic studies of the staff and staff work from the brigade major to the chief of staff at general headquarters. This is a large subject on which modern research is still in its infancy, but it is safe to predict that the staff officer's profile will be greatly enhanced. The public has for too long been entertained, but badly misled, by the antics of staff officers in *Oh What a Lovely War* (jumping over each other's backs) and the cowering incompetence of *Blackadder*'s Captain Kevin Darling.

Despite the surprisingly dismissive remarks of Sir John Keegan,[39] the most important topic of research and debate for the younger generation of military historians (and some not much younger than Keegan himself) is what is broadly described as 'the learning curve'. This involves the careful analysis of operations and lessons learned, in order to understand how the small, inexperienced, traditionally organized and under-equipped BEF of 1914 overcame the almost unbroken run of setbacks and disasters in 1914–16 to evolve into the highly efficient and successful force of the final phase of the war in 1917–18.

Traditional critics would argue that nothing did change: the German Army was worn down by attrition, lacked the manpower resources and production capacity to make good its losses and effectively defeated itself by prolonging its final, desperate offensives in 1918.

However sharply modern scholars may disagree among themselves, they would unite in rejecting these explanations as unsatisfactory and incomplete. Indeed the scholarly debate has already moved on to more specialized and specific issues such as: the basic nature of the problem, the origins and steepness of the 'learning curve', at what level innovations were introduced and how they were implemented by high command. Was Haig little more than a spectator in the final weeks or more akin to the conductor of an orchestra?

Tim Travers, in his book *The Killing Ground*, defined the problem in essentially managerial terms.[40] In his opinion the British Army suffered from a personalized and hierarchical command structure which inhibited initiative, and a complete lack of any command doctrine. Consequently, there was confusion between control and flexibility, commanders interfering in their subordinates' planning and operational spheres when they should have allowed initiative, and on other occasions failing to exert control when it was necessary. By contrast, Robin Prior and Trevor

Wilson see the problem in terms of a tactical and technical dilemma: how to combine artillery and infantry in 'bite
and hold' tactics which would allow the often successful
'break-ins' to the enemy's front trenches to be consolidated
and not driven out by counter-attacks. Both approaches
have advanced the discussion, but Prior and Wilson's has
attracted more followers, in part perhaps because Travers's
definition of traditional and modern weapons systems
placed artillery in the former (and therefore non-
progressive) category, whereas most scholars view artillery
as *the* vital innovative arm which provided the basis for a
revolution in military affairs (or RMA).[41] As Gary Sheffield
sums up this point, 'the fighting of 1914 looked back to the
era of Napoleon; the highly skilled BEF of 1918 used an
embryonic version of the modern all arms battle'.[42]

The British artillery's rapid development is remarkable
in the light of its deficiencies in 1914 when there was no high
explosive (HE) shell for the 18-pounder gun, no smoke or
gas shell, no creeping barrage, no apparatus to locate enemy guns and virtually no air observation. By late 1917, as
the opening of the battle of Cambrai demonstrated, most of
these defects had been overcome, and by a combination of
predicted fire, big guns, mortars, machineguns, tanks and
aircraft, the British had devised a method of dominating
the enemy's artillery and trench defences. The severe limi-
tation, which Haig and the high command were reluctant to
accept, was that no advance could safely be pushed beyond
the protection of one's own artillery. This was a prime factor in the steady advance in the final 'hundred days' when, it
has been suggested, logistical constraints rather than enemy
resistance was the chief cause of delays and slow progress.[43]

Similar innovations occurred in infantry organization
and tactics, displaying an impressive interaction of weapons
development and evolving doctrine. By mid-1918, for example, each division had three fewer battalions than in

1916 but battalions had much more formidable firepower. The four Lewis guns per battalion of 1916 had grown to thirty-six, plus eight light trench mortars and sixteen rifle-bombers.[44] The platoon structure was drastically changed to take full advantage of the increased firepower. By 1918 doctrinal lessons, embodied in 'Notes on Recent Fighting' were being issued and inculcated even while battles were in progress.

Paddy Griffith has gone furthest in arguing that these practical and doctrinal innovations, enhanced by sustained and vigorous training, were as impressive as anything produced by the German general staff.[45] By 1918, consequently, in a myriad of small unit actions, the British infantry was able to advance using its own weapons to overcome such enemy strongpoints as had survived the artillery barrage.

To sum up, between 1916 and 1918, albeit through trial and error and by no means always successfully, the BEF created a very effective weapons system combining infantry, armour, artillery (the battle winner *par excellence*) and machineguns assisted by airpower and wireless communications. By the start of the final 'hundred days' in 1918 the BEF (and its allies) had an abundance of weapons and munitions, impressive engineering and logistical back-up, and greatly improved command and staff work. Thus after a sluggish start and many slips, the 'learning curve' had risen sharply from late 1917 to produce a war machine to which the enemy had no answer.[46]

Robin Prior and Trevor Wilson have recently raised once again the question 'why are we so obsessed by the Great War of 1914-1918'?[47] It was not history's longest or bloodiest conflict. It was shorter than the Second World War and cost only one-fifth as many lives. The areas of wholesale devastation and destruction were limited. Indeed the military stalemate on the Western Front ensured that the armies lacked the opportunity to rampage widely over enemy territory, burning cities and destroying crops and livestock. They suggest that the main explanation lies in timing: after a relatively peaceful era the advent of war shattered illusions of improving international co-operation, economic development and the spread of liberal systems of government.

But for Britain there is clearly an additional reason. The view has persisted that approximately one million deaths in combat (in all war theatres) was an unacceptable catastrophe rather than the high price that had to be paid to safeguard the nation's strategic interests in western Europe and the empire. As we have seen, the nagging doubt has persisted, and been voiced again recently by Alan Clark, Niall Ferguson, John Charmley and other writers that Britain could and should have avoided involvement in a conflict which did not threaten its vital interests. Paul Fussell's influential book has reinforced the view that in literary and cultural terms the First World War lies 'outside history' and is unique in its dreadfulness.

The contrary argument by academic historians such as Prior and Wilson, and the other predominantly military historians discussed here, has an uphill struggle to reach a public brought up on 'the war poets' and abetted by newspapers and television programmes which, with honourable exceptions, tend to go on reinforcing the received images of horrendous conditions, unnecessary slaughter and ultimate futility. In these chapters I have challenged what I believe to be myths, misrepresentations or half-truths based on the views of a very small, unrepresentative minority, plainly at odds with the findings of a new generation of scholars who, at last – towards the end of the twentieth century – have got to grips with the First World War as history. It needs to be stressed that none of these historians – who include Australians, Canadians, New Zealanders and Americans as well as Britons – are militaristic or anti-democratic. Indeed, some have celebrated the

Allied Victory in 1918 as a vindication of liberal democracy over autocratic militarism. Perhaps, however, it is a mark of a civilized, liberal society that it hugs and cherishes its defeats, dwells obsessively on the worst combat conditions and on casualties, and cannot forgive Field Marshal Haig for being victorious.[48] Military historians nevertheless find these deep-rooted myths disturbing and are striving to dispel them, believing that they are not just narrow academic specialized issues, but have serious implications for our present attitudes and values and may well affect security decisions.

In the 1996 television programme reappraising the reputation of Sir Douglas Haig, John Hussey suggested it would take another fifty years to get the British achievement in the First World War understood and accepted as history. I too am pessimistic but I hope it will not take quite as long as that. I will conclude by quoting Ian Beckett's appropriate and rather more optimistic imagery in reviewing the work of military historians:

> It might be argued that we have broken the Hindenburg Line, we are somewhere around the end of October 1918 and we can see those green fields beyond. It is only a pity that, back in Blighty, it is still 1 July 1916. Clearly we need a superior breed of conducting officers when the war correspondents arrive to visit the 'Old Front Line'.[49]

Sir Lees Knowles (1857–1928)

Lees Knowles was a gentleman of independent means who devoted his life to public service and an impressive range of good causes. He was a man of tremendous energy and wide interests: an outstanding athlete, barrister, Member of Parliament, traveller, stalwart of the Territorial Army in Lancashire, benefactor of his school and college, and amateur military historian.

Lees Knowles came of old Lancashire families. His father, John, was High Sheriff of the county in 1892–3 and his mother, Elizabeth, was the daughter of James Lees of Green Bank, Oldham. Thus 'Lees Knowles' was his full name rather than the hyphenated surname which so often appears in publications deriving from the lectures which he endowed.

At Rugby School Lees Knowles had distinguished himself in athletics, and he added to his reputation at Cambridge. He ran against Oxford in the three-mile race in 1876, in the mile in the two following years, and in the quarter-mile in 1879. He became president of the Cambridge University Athletics Club and in 1901 took out a combined Oxford and

Cambridge team to compete against leading universities in Canada and the United States. For these services Oxford conferred on him the rare distinction of an honorary 'Dark Blue'. Athletics and other sports, including football, continued to interest him throughout his life.

After reading natural sciences at Trinity College he was admitted at Lincoln's Inn and was called to the Bar in 1882, joining the Northern Circuit the following year. His dominant interest was, however, in politics, where the drive towards public service far outweighed personal ambition. He was the Conservative Member of Parliament for West Salford from 1886 to 1906, losing his seat in the Liberal landslide in the latter year. He served as unpaid private secretary to C. T. Ritchie, first when the latter was President of the Local Government Board (1887–1892) and again when Ritchie was President of the Board of Trade (1895–1900). This experience he put to good effect as a member of various charitable bodies, including the Guinness Trust for Housing the Poor and the City of London Parochial Charities. He served on numerous committees and trusts supporting schools and hospitals, and his many benefactions included scholarships at Rugby School and Trinity College, and a grant of land at Pendleton as part of a municipal scheme to provide work for the unemployed.

Lees Knowles was also a fervent supporter of the Volunteer and Territorial movement in Lancashire. He was vice-chairman of the county's Territorial Army Association and at various times commanded the 3rd, 7th and 8th Battalions of the Lancashire Fusiliers which made important contributions in both the South African and First World Wars. In 1909 Lees Knowles commissioned a portrait of himself in the uniform of Colonel of the Volunteer Battalion Lancashire Fusiliers which still hangs at one of his former homes, Turton Tower, near Bolton.

Lees Knowles was an amateur military historian with a special interest in the Napoleonic era; indeed, he became an authority on Napoleon's exile in St Helena. His publications included a translation from the Italian of Antonio Farace's *The Taking of Capri 1806–1808*, an edition of the *Letters of Captain Englebert Lutyens, St Helena 1820–1823*, and, among his own works, *A Day with Corps Students in Germany*, and *The War in the Peninsula: Some Letters of Lt Robert Knowles*.

This energetic public servant, tireless committee member and champion of good causes appeared to be a confirmed bachelor, but in August 1915 (aged 58) he married Lady Nina Ogilvie-Grant, youngest daughter of the tenth Earl of Seafield. Two days after the wedding, at St Margaret's Westminster, the couple were involved in a horrific train accident near Weedon when the Holyhead express was derailed with the loss of nine lives. Though badly shaken, the Lees Knowles went ahead with their honeymoon in Ireland, returning to a touching welcome-home from their numerous servants and tenants. There were no children, so the baronetcy, granted in 1903, became extinct.

Doubtless through a combination of his personal interest in military history, devotion to the Lancashire Fusiliers and foreboding about the darkening international situation, on the last day of 1912 Sir Lees Knowles founded at Trinity College, Cambridge the 'Lectureship on Military Science' which, after nearly a century, continues to honour his memory.

The Lees Knowles lectures

I am most grateful to Boyd Hilton and Jonathan Smith for their help in compiling this list. There are some unavoidable gaps and anomalies for which there are three possible explanations. A few speakers were invited, and listed by the College Council, but did not deliver the lectures. Lecturers are appointed for the academic year but the lectures may be given in any of the three terms; consequently two series may appear to have been delivered in one year and none in the next. Since the late 1970s the lectures have usually been delivered in alternate years. Lastly, it should be noted that some of the lectures have been published under slightly different titles from those listed by Trinity College.

1915 J. S. Corbett	The great war after Trafalgar
1922 Col. Maxwell Earle	The principal strategical problems affecting the British Empire
1923 Col. Maxwell Earle	The principles of war
1924 Col. M. A. Wingfield	The eight principles as exemplified in the Palestine campaign, 1915–1918
Lt.-Col. F. P. Nosworthy	Russia before, during and after the Great War

1925 Maj.-Gen. Sir Frederick Maurice	Statesmen and soldiers in the American Civil War
1927 Maj.-Gen. Sir Wilkinson Bird	Some early crises of the war, and the events leading up to them, Western Front 1914
1928 Maj.-Gen. Sir George Aston	Problems of empire defence
1928 A. R. Hinks	Frontiers and boundary delimitations
1930 W. W. Tarn	Hellenistic military developments
1931 Adml. Sir Herbert Richmond	Capture at sea in war
1932 Capt. B. H. Liddell Hart	The movement of military thought from the eighteenth to the twentieth century, and its influence on European history
1933 John Buchan (Lord Tweedsmuir)	Oliver Cromwell as a soldier
1934 Air Commodore L. E. O. Charlton	Military aeronautics applied to modern warfare
1936 C. R. M. F. Cruttwell	The role of British strategy in the Great War, 1914–1918
1937 Gen. Sir Edmund Ironside	British military history from 1899 to the present day
1939 Gen. Sir Archibald Wavell	Generalship
1940 Gen. Sir Frederick Maurice	Public opinion in war
1941 Capt. Cyril Falls	The nature of modern warfare
1942 Maj.-Gen. Sir George Lindsay	The War on the civil and military fronts
1943 Adml. Lord Keyes	Combined operations and amphibious warfare
1944 Maj. Oliver Stewart	The tactical origins of air power
1945 Lord Hankey	The principles of government control in war
1946 Col. A. H. Burne	Military strategy as exemplified in the Second World War: a strategical examination of the land operations
1947 Air Marshal Sir Arthur Tedder	Air power in modern warfare
1948 Adml. Sir William James	The influence of sea power upon the history of the British people
1949 Gen. Sir Ronald Weeks	Organisation and equipment for war
1950 Sir Henry Tizard	The influence of war on science
1951 Gen. Sir William Platt	The campaign against Italian East Africa, 1940–41
1951 Capt. G. H. Roberts, RN	The battles of the Atlantic
1952 Air Chief Marshal Sir Roderic Hill	Some human factors in war
1953 Sir Fitzroy Maclean	Irregular warfare

1954 Gen. Sir Brian Horrocks	Are we training for the last war?
1956 Prof. P. M. S. Blackett	Atomic weapons, 1945–1955
1957 J. P. W. Ehrman	Cabinet government and war, 1890–1940
1958 Field Marshal Lord Harding	Mediterranean strategy in the Second World War
1958 Sir Leslie Rowan	Arms and economics, the changing challenge
1960 Capt. S. W. Roskill	Maritime strategy in the twentieth century
1961 Field Marshal Lord Slim	The military mind *and* The spirit of an army
1962 Gen. Sir John Hackett	The profession of arms
1963 Dr Noble Frankland	The strategic air offensive
1965 Sir Solly Zuckerman	Science and military affairs
1966 Prof. M. Howard	The conduct of British strategy in the Second World War
1968 Prof. R. V. Jones	Command
1969 Alastair Buchan	The changing functions of military force in international politics
1970 Prof. G. F. A. Best	Conscience and the conduct of war, from the French Revolution through the Franco-Prussian war
1971 Prof. F. H. Hinsley	War and the development of the international system
1972 Prof. J. Erickson	Soviet soldiers and Soviet society
1973 Prof. P. G. Mackesey	Problems of an amphibious power, 1795–1808
1974 D. C. Watt	European armed forces and the approach of the Second World War, 1933–1939
1974 Prof. H. Bondi	Science and defence
1975 Dr R.L. Clutterbuck	Guerrilla warfare and political violence
1977 Prof. C. Thorne	Anglo-American relations and the war against Japan, 1941–45
1979 Field Marshal Lord Carver	Apostles of mobility
1981 Prof. L. W. Martin	The evolution of nuclear strategic doctrine since 1945
1983 Alistair Horne	The French army and politics, 1870–1970
1985 Dr Geoffrey Parker	European warfare, 1520–1660
1987 John Keegan	Some fallacies of military history
1989 Dr Alan Bowman	Vindolanda and the Roman army: new documents from the northern frontier
1991 Maurice Keen	English military experience c. 1340–c. 1450
1993 Prof. William McNeill	Dance, drill and bonding in human affairs

1995 Prof. Hew Strachan	The politics of the British Army, 1815–1914
1997 Field Marshal Sir Peter Inge	Military force in a changing world
1999 Prof. Keith Jeffery	'For the freedom of small nations': Ireland and the Great War
2001 Prof. Brian Bond	Britain and the First World War: The challenge to historians

Notes

1 THE NECESSARY WAR, 1914–1918

1 Robin Prior and Trevor Wilson, 'The First World War', *Journal of Contemporary History*, 35, 2 (April 2000), 319–28.

2 Paul Kennedy, *The Rise of the Anglo-German Antagonism, 1860–1914* (London: Allen & Unwin, 1980), pp. 424–5.

3 Ibid., pp. 454–8. Michael Brock, 'Britain Enters the War', in R. J. W. Evans and H. P. Von Strandmann (eds.), *The Coming of the First World War* (Oxford: Clarendon Press, 1988), pp. 145–78.

4 Michael Howard, *The Continental Commitment* (London: Temple Smith, 1972), pp. 31–52.

5 Brock, 'Britain Enters the War', pp. 154–5.

6 Ibid., p. 161.

7 Kennedy, *Anglo-German Antagonism*, p. 461. Bentley B. Gilbert, 'Pacifist to Internationalist: David Lloyd George in 1911 and 1914', *Historical Journal*, 28, 4 (1985), 863–85.

8 Fritz Fischer, *Germany's Aims in the First World War* (London: Chatto & Windus 1967), pp. 103–6.

9 David French, *British Strategy and War Aims, 1914–1916* (London: Allen & Unwin, 1986), p. ix.

10 Ibid., p. xiii; Kennedy, *Anglo-German Antagonism*, p. 425. Howard, *Continental Commitment*, pp. 6–7.

11 Kennedy, *Anglo-German Antagonism*, pp. 469–70.

12 Brock, *Britain Enters the War*, p. 76. The Bosnian and Kosovo crises of 1992–5 and 1999 show that this crusading urge to restore civilized values is far from dead.

13 French, *British Strategy*, pp. xiii, 108, 111, 159.

14 David Stevenson, *The First World War and International Politics* (Oxford: Oxford University Press, 1988), pp. 103–6.

15 Ibid., pp. 106–13, 181–2, 201–1; Fischer, *Germany's Aims*, pp. 508–9.

16 J. M. Bourne, *Britain and the Great War 1914–1918* (London: Arnold, 1989), pp. 227–9.

17 Ibid., pp. 210, 229; Philip Dutton, 'Geschäft Uber Alles: notes on some medallions inspired by the sinking of the Lusitania', *Imperial War Museum Review*, (1986), 30–42.

18 Bourne, *Britain and the Great War*, pp. 207–8; Jane Carmichael, *First World War Photographs* (London: Routledge, 1989).

19 Nick Hiley, 'The News Media and British Propaganda, 1914–1918', in J. J. Becker and S. Audoin-Rouzeau (eds.), *Les Sociétés Européennes et la Guerre de 1914–1918* (Paris: Université de Paris X-Nanterre, 1990).

20 Ibid. See also Nick Hiley, '"Kitchener Wants You" and "Daddy what did *You* do in the Great War?": the myth of British recruiting posters', *Imperial War Museum Review*, 11 (1997), 40–58.

21 Michael Paris (ed.), *The First World War and Popular Cinema* (Edinburgh: Edinburgh University Press, 1999). See also Stuart Sillars, *Art and Survival in First World War Britain* (London: Macmillan, 1987), esp. pp. 116–31; Nicholas Reeves, 'Through the Eye of the Camera: Contemporary Cinema Audiences and their "Experience" of War in the Film Battle of the Somme', in Hugh Cecil and Peter H. Liddle (eds.), *Facing Armageddon: The First World War Experienced* (London: Leo Cooper, 1996), pp. 780–98; and Stephen Badsey, Introduction, Roger Smither (ed.), *Imperial War Museum Film Catalogue*, Volume I: *The First World War Archive* (London: Flicks Books, 1994).

22 Gary Sheffield, 'The Morale of the British Army on the Western Front, 1914–1918', Occasional Papers 2, ISWS De Montfort University (1995), p. 5. See also G. D. Sheffield, *Leadership in the Trenches* (London: Macmillan, 2000), Passim.

23 Gary Sheffield, 'Officer–Man Relations, Discipline and Morale in the British Army of the Great War', in Cecil and Liddle, *Facing Armageddon*, pp. 413–24. There were also some 'combat refusals' by Australian troops in 1918 due to exhaustion.

24 John Peaty, 'Haig and Military Discipline', in Brian Bond and Nigel Cave (eds.), *Haig: A Reappraisal Seventy Years On* (Barnsley: Pen & Sword, 1999), pp. 196–222.

25 Gary Sheffield, '"Oh What a Futile War!": representations of the Western Front in modern British media and popular culture', in Ian Stewart and Susan Carruthers (eds.), *War, Culture and the Media* (London: Flicks Books, 1996), p. 59.

26 Pat Barker, *The Regeneration Trilogy* (Penguin Books, 1997), and the film *Regeneration* (1997).

27 Jean Moorcroft Wilson, *Siegfried Sassoon. The Making of a War Poet. A Biography 1886–1918* (London: Duckworth, 1998), pp. 291–6, 318–19, 341, 367.

28 Ibid., pp. 373–4.

29 Ibid., pp. 315, 353, 386. See also S. Sassoon, *Siegfried's Journey* (London: Faber & Faber, paperback edn, 1982 [1945]) p. 57.

30 See, for example, Robin Prior and Trevor Wilson, *Command on the Western Front* (Oxford: Blackwell, 1992), and Peter Simkins, 'Somme Reprise', in Brian Bond et al., *Look to Your Front: Studies in the First World War* (Staplehurst: Spellmount, 1999) pp. 147–62.

31 See, for example, Gary Sheffield's robust counter-attack in '"Oh What a Futile War!"'. On GHQ's relations with the press see Stephen Badsey, 'Haig and the Press', in Bond and Cave, *Haig, A Reappraisal*, pp. 176–95.

32 Sheffield, '"Oh What a Futile War!"', pp. 59–60; Bourne, *Britain and the Great War*, pp. 221–3.

33 John Keegan, *The Face of Battle* (London: Cape, 1976), p. 272. Sheffield, '"Oh What a Futile War!"', p. 60; Bourne, *Britain and the Great War*, pp. 222–3.

34 See especially Ian Beckett and Keith Simpson (eds.), *A Nation in Arms* (Manchester: Manchester University Press, 1985).

35 John Keegan, *The First World War* (London: Pimlico, 1999), p. 315.

36 Brian Bond, 'A Victory Worse than a Defeat? British Interpretations of the First World War', Liddell Hart Lecture, King's College, London (1997), p. 2.

37 Peter Dennis and Jeffrey Grey (eds.), *1918: Defining Victory* (Canberra: Department of Defence, 1999), pp. 38–9.

38 Trevor Wilson, *The Myriad Faces of War* (Cambridge: Polity Press, 1986), p. 586.

39 Sheffield, '"Oh What a Futile War!"', p. 60. See also Jonathan Bailey, 'The First World War and the Birth of Modern Warfare',

Strategic and Combat Studies Institute, Occasional Papers 22 (Camberley, 1996).

40 Ben Pimlott, *Hugh Dalton* (London: Faber, 1985), p. 253. Cited as an epigraph by Bourne, *Britain and the Great War*, p. 225.

41 Stevenson, *First World War*, p. 308ff. David French, *The Strategy of the Lloyd George Coalition, 1916–1918* (Oxford: Clarendon Press, 1995), pp. 293–7.

42 Wilson, *The Myriad Faces of War*, pp. 848–51.

43 French, *The Strategy of the Lloyd George Coalition* pp. 296–7.

44 Bourne, *Britain and the Great War*, pp. 205–6, 230–1.

45 Jay Winter, *The Great War and the British People* (Cambridge: Cambridge University Press, 1985), pp. 71–99.

46 See, for example, Jay Winter, *Sites of Memory, Sites of Mourning: The Great War in European Cultural History* (Cambridge: Cambridge University Press, 1995), and Adrian Gregory, *The Silence of Memory: Armistice Day 1919–1946* (Oxford: Berg, 1994).

47 Modris Eksteins, *Rites of Spring: The Great War and the Birth of the Modern Age* (London: Bantam, 1989), pp. 255–6.

48 Thirty-eight 'Thankful Villages' are believed to have had no fatalities, and one Somerset village, Stocklinch, had none in the Second World War either. See correspondence in *The Times*, 15 and 20 November 1997. See also Ian F. W. Beckett *The Great War 1914–1918* (London: Longman, 2001), p. 439.

49 Eksteins, *Rites of Spring*, p. 297.

2 GOODBYE TO ALL THAT, 1919–1933

1 Correlli Barnett, 'A military historian's view of the Literature of the Great War', *Transactions of the Royal Society of Literature*, 36 (1970), 1–18. See also Barnett's *The Collapse of British Power* (London: Eyre Methuen, 1972) pp. 424–35.

2 Martin Stephen, *The Price of Pity* (London: Leo Cooper, 1996), pp. 138–47.

3 Rosa Maria Bracco, *Merchants of Hope. British Middlebrow Writers and the First World War, 1919–1939* (Oxford: Berg, 1993).

4 Hugh Cecil, 'British War Novelists', in Cecil and Liddle, *Facing Armageddon*, p. 803.

5 Brian Bond, 'Anti-War Writers and their Critics', ibid., pp. 820–1. See also Keith Grieves, 'C. E. Montague and the Making of Disenchantment, 1914–1921', *War in History*, 4, 1 (1997), 35–9; and Grieves, 'C. E. Montague, Manchester and the Remembrance

of War, 1918–1925', *Bulletin of the John Rylands University Library of Manchester*, 77, 2 (Summer 1995), 85–104.

6 Robert Wohl, *The Generation of 1914* (London: Weidenfeld & Nicolson, 1980), p. 219.

7 Bond, 'Anti-War Writers', p. 825; Cyril Falls, *War Books, a Critical Guide* (London: P. Davies, 1930), p. 292.

8 Hugh Cecil, *The Flower of Battle: British Fiction Writers of the First World War* (London: Secker & Warburg, 1995), pp. 18, 24, 35.

9 Falls, *War Books*, p. 208; Alfred Oliver Pollard, *Fire-Eater: the Memoirs of a V.C.* (London: Hutchinson, 1932).

10 Wilson, *Siegfried Sassoon*, pp. 291, 312, 341, 367; Robert Graves, *But It Still Goes On, an Accumulation* (London: Cape, 1930), p. 13.

11 Adrian Caesar, *Taking It Like a Man: Suffering, Sexuality and the War Poets* (Manchester: Manchester University Press, 1990). On Herbert Read see Cecil, *Flower of Battle*, pp. 244–66.

12 Guy Chapman, *A Kind of Survivor* (London: Gollancz, 1975), pp. 158–9, 280. Anthony Eden, Earl of Avon, *Another World, 1897–1917* (London: Allen Lane, 1976), p. 150.

13 Charles Edmonds [Charles Carrington], *A Subaltern's War* (London: P. Davis, 1929) pp. 194–5, 206–8; Sir David Kelly, *The Ruling Few or the Human Background to Diplomacy* (London: Hollis & Carter, 1952), pp. 86–108. I owe the latter reference to Professor Paul Smith.

14 Falls, *War Books*, preface, pp. i, xi.

15 Graves, *But It Still Goes On*, pp. 16–17, 41–3; Robert Graves, *In Broken Images: Selected Letters of Robert Graves 1914–1946*, ed. Paul O'Prey. (London: Hutchinson, 1982), p. 286.

16 Bracco, *Merchants of Hope*, pp. 149–53, 178, 185–6.

17 Falls, *War Books*, p. 261, noted that Henri Barbusse's *Under Fire*, trans. Fitzwater Wray (London: Dent, 1917) had sold more copies than any book except Remarque's. He described it as 'frank anti-war propaganda and very unreal'.

18 Modris Eksteins, 'All Quiet on the Western Front and the Fate of a War', *Journal of Contemporary History*, 15 (1980), 345–66; and Eksteins, *Rites of Spring* pp. 276–90. The late Dirk Bogarde chose *All Quiet* as his 'Book of the Century', concluding that 'no one has better explained the fate of the ordinary man engaged incomprehendingly in the viciousness, uselessness and utter waste of war' (*Daily Telegraph*, 6 March 1999). One wonders, then, why he volunteered to serve in the (pointless) Second World War.

19 The publisher, Peter Davies, virtually kidnapped the dilatory author Frederic Manning and held him captive until he had completed what turned out to be his masterpiece, *The Middle Parts of Fortune*. Jonathan Marwil, *Frederic Manning, An Unfinished Life* (Durham, NC: Duke University Press, 1988), p. 254.

20 Erich Maria Remarque, *All Quiet on the Western Front* (London: Putnam, August 1929, 18th reprint since publication in March), p. 287.

21 Eksteins, *Rites of Spring*, pp. 282, 298. In analysing 'the Failure of the War Books' Herbert Read felt that even Remarque's effort was flawed: Remarque's depiction of war and suffering had its own sadistic attractions. See Read, *A Coat of Many Colours* (1945).

22 Eksteins, *Rites of Spring*, pp. 295-6.

23 Modris Eksteins, 'War, Memory, and Politics: the Fate of the Film *All Quiet on the Western Front*', *Central European History*, 13, 1 (March 1980), 60-82.

24 Paris, *The First World War and Popular Cinema*, pp. 53, 55, 60.

25 Ibid., pp. 52, 61. In his introduction (p. 2) Paris disputes Samuel Hynes's assertion that literature has been the main influence in shaping popular memory of the Great War. 'Today ... for those generations who have no direct experience of war, the cinema screen provides their dominant impression of what "war" is.'

26 Samuel Hynes, *A War Imagined: The First World War and English Culture* (London: Bodley Head, 1990), p. 455.

27 Eksteins, *Rites of Spring*, pp. 290-1.

28 Ian Beckett, 'Frocks and Brasshats', in Brian Bond (ed.), *The First World War and British Military History*, (Oxford: Clarendon Press, 1991), pp. 91-3.

29 Keith Grieves, 'Early Historical Responses to the Great War: Fortescue, Conan Doyle, and Buchan', ibid., pp. 26-9.

30 Ibid., pp. 30-9, and Keith Grieves, '*Nelson's History of the War*: John Buchan as a Contemporary Historian, 1915-1922', *Journal of Contemporary History*, 28, 3 (July 1993), 533-51.

31 Robin Prior, *Churchill's 'World Crisis' as History* (London: Croom Helm, 1983). On Haig's comments on the book in draft see pp. 261-9. Sir Martin Gilbert identified Arthur Balfour as responsible for the witticism about *The World Crisis*, and Paul Addison located the source – Blanche E. C. Dugdale, *Arthur James Balfour* (London: Hutchinson 1939), II, p. 247.

32 Beckett, 'Frocks and Brasshats', pp. 94-7. In December 1921 Churchill wrote to his wife 'It is a great chance to put my whole case in an agreeable form to an attentive audience. And the pelf will make us very comfortable'.

33 Winston S. Churchill, *The World Crisis, 1911–1918*, 2 vols. (London: Odhams, 1938) pp. 946–7, 1070–93, 1213, 1374–5, 1384–5.

34 Prior, *Churchill's 'World Crisis'*, pp. 226–9, 279–83. See also Lord Sydenham *The World Crisis by Winston Churchill: a criticism by Lord Sydenham and others* (London: Hutchinson, nd [1927]).

35 Brian Bond, 'A Victory Worse than a Defeat?' Liddell Hart Lecture, King's College London (1997), p. 8.

36 See Hew Strachan, '"The Real War": Liddell Hart, Cruttwell and Falls', and Brian Holden Reid, 'T. E. Lawrence and his Biographers', in Bond, *The First World War and British Military History*; See also Brian Bond, 'Liddell Hart and the First World War', in Brian Bond et al., *Look to your Front*, pp. 13–24.

37 David Lloyd George, *War Memoirs*, 2 vols. (London: Odhams, 1938), Foreword, pp. v–vi, 2011. David French has shown that Haig did, indeed, present his own case in the 1920s, albeit indirectly, through others' publications – 'Sir Douglas Haig's Reputation, 1918–1928: A Note', *Historical Journal*, 28, 4, (1985), 953–60.

38 This selection was quoted in my Liddell Hart Lecture, pp. 8–9.

39 George W. Egerton, 'The Lloyd George War Memoirs: A Study in the Politics of Memory', *Journal of Modern History*, 60 (March 1988), 55–94, esp. 77–81, 90.

40 Hynes, *A War Imagined*, p. 439. See ibid., p. 452, for Douglas Jerrold's summary of the 'lie' about the war.

3 DONKEYS AND FLANDERS MUD: THE WAR REDISCOVERED IN THE 1960s

1 Philip Larkin, *High Windows* (London: Faber, 1979), p. 34.

2 Arthur Marwick, *Britain in the Century of Total War* (Harmondsworth: Penguin, 1970), pp. 455–6.

3 Brian Bond, *The Pursuit of Victory. From Napoleon to Saddam Hussain* (Oxford: Oxford University Press, 1996), pp. 188–9. Arthur Marwick, *The Sixties: Cultural Revolution in Britain, France, Italy and the United States c. 1958–1974* (Oxford: Oxford University Press, 1998), pp. 533–63, 632–42.

4 I owe this information to Professor Robert O'Neill.

5 Matthew Richardson, 'A Changing Meaning for Armistice Day', in Peter Liddle and Hugh Cecil (eds.), *At the Eleventh Hour: Reflections, Hopes and Anxieties at the Closing of the Great War, 1918* (London: Leo Cooper, 1998), pp. 356–60.

6 Alex Danchev, '"Bunking" and Debunking', in Bond, *The First World War*, p. 270; and see pp. viii–ix for a chronological list of publications.

7 John Grigg, 'Nobility and War. The Unselfish Commitment?' *Encounter*, March 1990, pp. 21–7.

8 See Hew Strachan, '"The Real War": Liddell Hart, Cruttwell and Falls', in Bond, *The First World War*, pp. 41–67. Brian Bond, 'Liddell Hart and *The First World War*', in Bond, *Look To Your Front*, pp. 13–24.

9 Danchev, '"Bunking" and Debunking', p. 282. For Raymond Fletcher's links with the Soviet and Czechoslovak secret services (KGB and StB) see Christopher Andrew and Vasili Mitrokhin, *The Mitrokhin Archive. The KGB in Europe and the West* (Harmondsworth: Penguin, 2000) pp. 526–7.

10 Danchev '"Bunking" and Debunking', pp. 264–6.

11 Brian Bond, 'Passchendaele: Verdicts, Past and Present', in Peter H. Liddle (ed.), *Passchendaele in Perspective* (London: Leo Cooper, 1997), pp. 481–7.

12 Alan Clark, *The Donkeys* (London: Hutchinson, 1961), pp. 180, 183, 186.

13 Michael Howard's review was published in the *Listener*, 3 August 1961.

14 Danchev, '"Bunking" and Debunking', p. 263, and Keith Simpson, 'The Reputation of Sir Douglas Haig', in Bond, *The First World War*, p. 156.

15 Taylor–Liddell Hart correspondence, Liddell Hart Centre for Military Archives, LH 1/676 Liddell Hart to Taylor 1 March and 25 May 1962.

16 A. J. P. Taylor, *The First World War. An Illustrated History* (London: Hamish Hamilton, 1963), pp. 13, 146, 148. The volume is dedicated to Joan Littlewood.

17 Ibid., pp. 24, 63, 79, 81.

18 Ibid., p. 220.

19 Taylor to Liddell Hart, 4 October 1962, LH1/676.

20 Taylor, *The First World War*, pp. 99–105.

21 Brian Bond, 'The Somme in British History', in Geoffrey Jensen and Andrew Wiest (eds.), *War in the Age of Technology. Myriad Faces of Modern Armed Conflict* (New York: New York University Press, 2001), pp. 194–210.

22 *Oh What a Lovely War* (Methuen, 1965), pp. 46, 49, 83.

23 General Sir Anthony Farrar-Hockley to the author, 19 April 2000.

24 Derek Paget, 'Remembrance Play: *Oh What a Lovely War* and History', in Tony Howard and John Stokes (eds.), *Acts of War: The Representation of Military Conflict on the British Stage and Television Since 1945* (Aldershot: Scolar, 1996), p. 83. On p. 95 Paget erroneously states that Alan Clark had been Liddell Hart's pupil at university.

25 Ibid. pp. 86–9. I am indebted to Stephen Badsey for drawing my attention to this illuminating essay.

26 Liddell Hart letter to the *Observer*, 20 June 1963 in Liddell Hart Papers LH13/61.

27 Typescript of Correlli Barnett's talk on the Third Programme 10 July 1963 in LH 13/61.

28 Brian Bond, 'A Victory Worse than a Defeat?' Liddell Hart Lecture, King's College London, 1997, p. 12. This paragraph draws heavily on Danchev, '"Bunking" and Debunking', p. 285.

29 See Danchev, '"Bunking" and Debunking', p. 286 for a brilliant evocation of the film's conclusion.

30 Copies of all the reviews mentioned are to be found in LH 13/61.

31 Peter Simkins, 'Everyman at War', in Bond, *The First World War*, p. 289.

32 Danchev, '"Bunking" and Debunking', p. 279.

33 Noble Frankland, *History at War: the Campaigns of an Historian* (London: Giles de la Mare, 1998), pp. 184–5.

34 LH 13/62 '1964 Great War Series on Television'.

35 Bond, "A Victory Worse than a Defeat". p. 11. For Audience Research Reports on the series see Danchev, '"Bunking" and Debunking', pp. 280–1.

36 See Simkins 'Everyman at War', pp. 289–313.

37 Brian Bond, 'Introduction', Bond, *The First World War*, p. 9.

38 Cuttings of A. J. P. Taylor's review of Terraine's *Douglas Haig* in the *Observer*, Michael Howard's in the *Sunday Times* and Alistair Horne's in the *Sunday Telegraph* (all 21 April 1963) are to be found in LH 1/683. On p. 235 of his book, in a 'Note on Casualties', Terraine made what could be construed as a critical reference to Liddell Hart's files on the subject which he had examined on one day only (11 June 1960). Liddell Hart defended his position in two letters to *The Times* (24 and 26 April 1963) and the correspondence came to an abrupt end. On the substantive point at issue Liddell Hart was right: the official figures provided by the official historian, Sir James Edmonds, were not reliable. See LH 1/683.

39 Michael Welch, 'Pangloss, John Terraine and the Western Front' (unpublished draft article).

40 Danchev, '"Bunking" and Debunking', p. 287. The gruesome
   statistics are taken from the published text of *Oh What a Lovely
   War*, p. 86.

4 THINKING THE UNTHINKABLE: THE FIRST WORLD
WAR AS HISTORY

1 London: Alan Sutton.
2 London: Viking.
3 Ian Beckett, 'Revisiting the Old Front Line', *Stand To!* 43 (April
   1995).
4 R. Prior and T. Wilson, 'Paul Fussell at War', *War in History*, 1, 1
   (1994), 63–80. They conclude: 'Any notion that the
   English-speaking people fought the Great War for a valid purpose,
   and at the last displayed greater military competence than their
   adversaries, has yet to find a place in modern memory.'
5 Stephen Badsey '*Blackadder Goes Forth* and the "Two Western
   Fronts" Debate', in Graham Roberts and Philip M. Taylor (eds.),
   Television and History (University of Luton Press, 2001),
   pp. 113–25. I am very grateful to Stephen Badsey for letting me
   read this essay before publication. However, he does not claim to
   have coined the term 'two Western Fronts'.
6 Niall Ferguson, *The Pity of War* (Luton: University of Luton
   Press, 1998), p. xxxi.
7 Badsey, '*Blackadder Goes Forth*'.
8 Hugh Brogan, 'The Great War and Rudyard Kipling', *Kipling
   Journal*, 72, 286 (June 1998), 21.
9 David Horspool, 'Remember the rats?' *Times Literary Supplement*,
   1 October 1999. Similar criticisms have been made about Nick
   Whitby's play *To the Green Fields Beyond*, see reviews in *Daily
   Telegraph*, 27 September 2000, and *Times Literary Supplement*,
   13 October 2000.
10 'Oh What a Lovely Tour', *Daily Telegraph*, 7 March 1998.
11 'Resonant anthem for doomed youth', *Daily Telegraph*,
   19 September 1998.
12 Badsey, '*Blackadder Goes Forth*'. Dick Rayner, 'The Sandringhams
   at Suvla Bay', *Stand To!* April 2000, pp. 5–9.
13 I am grateful to Robin Brodhurst for lending me the audio-visual
   cassette of the programme, and to the Reverend Nigel Cave for the
   reviews.
14 Ferguson, *The Pity of War*, p. xxxii. Nigel Cave, '*Timewatch* – a
   Review', *Haig Fellowship*, 3(1997).

15 John Peaty, 'Haig and Military Discipline', in Brian Bond and Nigel Cave (eds.), *Haig: a Reappraisal 70 Years On* (Barnsley: Pen and Sword; 1999), pp. 196–222.

16 Hansard, 'Review of Cases of Servicemen executed during the First World War', House of Commons Debates, vol. 316, cols. 1372–86, 24 July 1998. I am indebted to Keith Simpson MP for sending me these reports. John Hughes-Wilson 'The New Contemptibles', *The Spectator*, 3 June 2000. See also Cathryn Corns and John Hughes-Wilson, *Blindfold and Alone: British Military Executions in the Great War* (London: Cassell, 2001).

17 Those named were Julian Putkowski, Norman Stone, Alan Clark and Niall Ferguson.

18 A. N. Wilson in the *Sunday Telegraph*, 7 May 2000.

19 Max Hastings in the *Evening Standard* 27 February 1999. Discussed by Badsey, *'Blackadder Goes Forth'*.

20 See pp. 65–6.

21 Badsey, *'Blackadder Goes Forth'*. Schools in the Manchester area using *Blackadder* as their main history text were named at a conference on the First World War at Salford University, 12–13 May 2000.

22 Ian Beckett 'The Military Historian and the Popular Image of the Western Front, 1914–1918', *The Historian* (spring 1997). Sheffield, 'Oh What a Futile War', p. 63.

23 Information from Robin Brodhurst, who has a wide experience of examining on this subject. I am also indebted to Keith Grieves for sending me a comprehensive guide to the sources available to teachers on the First World War, including BBC Education's *History File: World War One*.

24 Western Front Association, *Bulletin*, 57 (June 2000).

25 'Behind the Lines', *Daily Telegraph*, 27 February 1999. Niall Ferguson in *The Pity of War* points out that of 103 complete poems in Owen's collected works only 31 can really be classified as anti-war (p. 448).

26 Gill Minikin 'Pride and delight: Motivating pupils through poetic writing about the First World War', *Teaching History*, 95 (May 1999), 32–7. Robin Brodhurst kindly sent me a copy of this issue. See also the issue for November 1999 – 'Doomed Youth: using theatre to support teaching about the First World War', 28–33.

27 Matthew Richardson, 'A Changing Meaning for Armistice Day', in Liddle and Cecil, *At the Eleventh Hour*, pp. 362–3; Brogan, 'The Great War and Rudyard Kipling', 19.

28 Richardson, 'A Changing Meaning', p. 360. Kathy Stevenson kindly supplied me with information about WFA membership numbers.

29 Richard Holmes, *The Western Front* (London: BBC Publications, 1999).

30 See, for example, Adrian Gregory, *The Silence of Memory. Armistice Day 1919–1946* (Oxford: Berg, 1994); S. Audoin-Rouzeau, *Men at War 1914–1918: National Sentiment and Trench Journalism in France during the First World War* (Oxford: Berg, 1992). Nicola Lambourne, 'First World War propaganda and the use and abuse of historic monuments on the Western Front', *IWM Review*, 12, 96–108.

31 Peter Simkins, *Kitchener's Army* (Manchester: Manchester University Press, 1988) and Simkins, 'Everyman at War' in Bond, *The First World War*. See also Beckett, 'Revisiting the Old Front Line'.

32 John Keegan set an unfortunate example in his celebrated book *The Face of Battle* (London: Cape, 1976) by concentrating on the first day of the battle of the Somme.

33 Oxford: Clarendon Press, 1997.

34 Gary Sheffield, 'The Morale of the British Army on the Western Front, 1914–1918', De Montfort University Bedford, ISWS Occasional Papers 2, 1995, and Beckett, 'Revisiting the Old Front Line'. G. D. Sheffield, *Leadership in the Trenches* (London: Macmillan was published in October 2000, after completion of the lectures on which this book is based.

35 Peter Simkins, 'Haig and his Army Commanders', in Bond and Cave, *Haig: a Reappraisal*, pp. 78–106.

36 John Bourne 'The BEF's Generals on 29 September 1918', in Dennis and Grey, *1918: Defining Victory*; idem, 'British Generals in the First World War' in G. D. Sheffield (ed.), *Leadership and Command* (London: Brassey's 1997) pp. 93–116.

37 Frank Davies and Gordon Maddocks, *Bloody Red Tabs: General Officer Casualties of the Great War, 1914–1918* (London: Leo Cooper, 1995), pp. xii, 22–4.

38 Peter Simkins, 'Co-Stars or Supporting Cast? British Divisions in the "Hundred Days", 1918', in Paddy Griffith (ed.), *British Fighting Methods in The Great War* (London: Frank Cass; 1996), pp. 50–69; Gary Sheffield, 'How even was the learning curve? Reflections on the British and Dominion Armies on the Western Front, 1916–1918', Conference Paper, University of Ottawa, May 2000. I am most grateful for an early view of this paper. John Lee,

'The SHLM Project – Assessing the Battle Performance of British Divisions', in Griffith, *British Fighting Methods*, pp. 175–81.

39 Keegan, *The First World War*, pp. 315–16, 472.

40 See Ian Beckett's stimulating discussion in 'The Military Historian and the Popular Image of the Western Front'.

41 Compare and contrast Tim Travers, *How The War Was Won* (London: Routledge, 1992), pp. 145–82, and Jonathan Bailey, 'British Artillery in the Great War' in Griffith, *British Fighting Methods*, pp. 23–49.

42 Sheffield, 'Oh What a Futile War', pp. 59–60.

43 Griffith, *British Fighting Methods*, pp. 17–18; R. Prior and T. Wilson, 'Winning the War' in Dennis and Grey, *1918: Defining Victory*, pp. 33–42, and G. Sheffield, 'The Indispensible Factor: the Performance of British Troops in 1918', ibid., pp. 72–95, 83–4.

44 Sheffield, 'The Indispensible Factor', pp. 85–6. I am grateful to Colonel Terry Cave for correcting my figures on battalion numbers and weaponry in 1918.

45 Paddy Griffith, *Battle Tactics of the Western Front* (Newhaven: Yale University Press, 1994).

46 Sheffield, 'How even was the learning curve?'

47 Review article, 'The First World War', *Journal of Contemporary History*, 35, 2 (April 2000), 319–28. This brief review conveys clear and critical comments on current historical judgements on the First World War in the light of John Keegan's and Niall Ferguson's books mentioned above.

48 Kevin Myers, 'We made a villain of a winner', *Sunday Telegraph*, 9 August 1998. Commenting on the predictable failure to commemorate the outstanding British and dominions' victory at Amiens on 8 August 1918, Myers concluded: 'Douglas Haig will always remain a demon. He above all others won the Great War; and for depriving them of a great defeat, the British will never forgive him.'

49 Beckett, 'Revisiting the Old Front Line'.

Select bibliography

Barnett, Correlli, *The Collapse of British Power*, (London: Eyre Methuen, 1972)

Beckett, Ian F. W. *The Great War, 1914–1918* (Harlow and New York: Longman, 2001)

Beckett, Ian F. W. and Simpson, Keith (eds.), *A Nation in Arms* (Manchester: Manchester University Press, 1985)

Bidwell, Shelford and Graham, Dominick, *Five-power: British Army Weapons and Theories of War 1904–1945* (London: Allen & Unwin, 1982)

Bond, Brian et al., *Look to Your Front: Studies in the First World War* (Staplehurst: Spellmount, 1999)

Bond, Brian (ed.), *The First World War and British Military History* (Oxford: Clarendon Press, 1991)

Bond, Brian, and Cave Nigel (eds.), *Haig: a Reappraisal Seventy Years On* (Barnsley: Pen & Sword, 1999)

Bourne, John M., *Britain and the Great War, 1914–1918* (London: Arnold, 1989)

Bracco, Rosa Maria, *Merchants of Hope: British Middlebrow Writers and the First World War, 1919–1939* (Oxford: Berg, 1993)

Caesar, Adrian, *Taking It Like a Man: Suffering, Sexuality and the War Poets* (Manchester: Manchester University Press, 1990)

Cecil, Hugh, *The Flower of Battle: British Fiction Writers of the First World War* (London: Secker & Warburg, 1995)

Cecil, Hugh and Liddle, Peter (eds.), *Facing Armageddon. The First World War Experienced* (London: Leo Cooper, 1996)

Davies, Frank and Maddocks, Graham, *Bloody Red Tabs: General Officer Casualties of the Great War, 1914–1918* (London: Leo Cooper, 1995)

Dennis, Peter and Grey, Jeffrey (eds.), *1918: Defining Victory* (Canberra: Department of Defence, 1999)

Edmonds, Charles [Charles Carrington], *A Subaltern's War* (London: Peter Davies, 1929)

Eksteins, Modris, *Rites of Spring: The Great War and the Birth of the Modern Age* (London: Bantam Press, 1989)

Ferguson, Niall, *The Pity of War* (London: Allen Lane, 1998)

French, David, *British Strategy and War Aims, 1914–1916* (London: Allen & Unwin, 1986)

French, David, *The Strategy of the David Lloyd George Coalition, 1916–1918* (Oxford: Clarendon Press, 1995)

Fussell, Paul, *The Great War and Modern Memory* (Oxford University Press, 1975)

Graves, Robert, *Goodbye to All That* (London: Cassell, 1957 [1929])

Gregory, Adrian, *The Silence of Memory. Armistice Day 1919–1946* (Oxford: Berg, 1994)

Griffith, Paddy, *Battle Tactics of the Western Front* (Newhaven: Yale University Press, 1994)

Griffith, Paddy, (ed.), *British Fighting Methods in the Great War* (London: Frank Cass, 1996)

Holmes, Richard, *The Western Front* (London: BBC Publications, 1999)

Howard, Michael, *The Continental Commitment* (London: Temple Smith, 1972)

Hynes, Samuel, *A War Imagined: The First World War and English Culture* (London: Bodley Head, 1990)

Keegan, John, *The First World War* (London: Pimlico, 1999)

Kelly, David V., *39 Months with the "Tigers", 1915–1918* (London: Ernest Benn, 1930)

Kennedy, Paul, *The Rise of the Anglo-German Antagonism, 1860–1914* (London: Allen & Unwin, 1980)

Liddle, Peter H. (ed), *Passchendaele in Perspective* (London: Leo Cooper, 1997)

Liddle, Peter and Cecil, Hugh (eds.), *At the Eleventh Hour: Reflections, Hopes and Anxieties at the Closing of the Great War, 1918* (London: Leo Cooper, 1995)

Marwick, Arthur, *Britain in the Century of Total War* (Harmondsworth: Penguin, 1970)

Middlebrook, Martin, *The First Day on the Somme, 1 July 1916* (London: Allen Lane, 1971)

Paris, Michael (ed.), *The First World War and Popular Cinema, 1914 to the Present* (Edinburgh: Edinburgh University Press, 1999)

Prior, Robin, *Churchill's 'World Crisis' as History* (London: Croom Helm, 1983)

Prior, Robin and Wilson, Trevor, *Command on the Western Front* (Oxford: Blackwell, 1992)

Sheffield, Gary, *Forgotten Victory. The First World War: Myths and Realities* (London: Headline, 2001)

Sheffield, Gary, *Leadership in the Trenches* (London: Macmillan, 2000)

Sheffield, Gary (ed.), *Leadership and Command* (London: Brassey's, 1997)

Sillars, Stuart, *Art and Survival in First World War Britain* (London: Macmillan, 1987)

Simkins, Peter, *Kitchener's Army* (Manchester: Manchester University Press, 1988)

Stephen, Martin, *The Price of Pity* (London: Leo Cooper, 1996)

Stevenson, David, *The First World War and International Politics* (Oxford: Oxford University Press, 1988)

Taylor, A. J. P., *The First World War. An Illustrated History* (London: Hamish Hamilton, 1963)

Travers, T. H. E., *The Killing Ground* (London: Allen & Unwin, 1987)

Travers, T. H. E., *How the War was Won* (London: Routledge, 1992)

Wilson, Jean Moorcroft, *Siegfried Sassoon. The Making of a War Poet* (London: Duckworth, 1998)

Wilson, Trevor, *The Myriad Faces of War* (Cambridge: Polity Press, 1986)

Winter, Jay, *The Great War and the British People* (Cambridge: Cambridge University Press, 1985)

Wohl, Robert, *The Generation of 1914* (London: Weidenfeld & Nicolson, 1980)

Index

Albert, King of the Belgians, 4
Aldington, Richard, writer, 30–1
All Quiet on the Western Front, book, 36–7, 77;
   film, 37–8, 40, 67
Allsop, Kenneth, writer, 67
Amiens, Battle of, 21
Armistice Day, 54, 89–90
Asquith, Herbert, Prime Minister, 3–5, 10
Attenborough, Richard, producer and
   director, 66–7

Baader-Meinhof Gang, 53
Badsey, Stephen, historian, 77, 86–7, 92
Balfour, A. J., statesman, 42
Barbusse, Henri, writer, 37
Barker, Pat, novelist, 76–7
Barnett, Correlli, historian, 27, 48, 59, 66, 69,
   81–2
Beaverbrook, Max, politician and newspaper
   proprietor, 18
Beckett, Ian, historian, 87, 92, 101
Belgium, 4–5, 8, 10
Belsen, concentration camp, 56
Bethell, Major-General H. K., 95
Bethmann Hollweg, Theobald von,
   Chancellor of Germany, 5, 8
Bettinson, Helen, television producer, 78–80
Blackadder Goes Forth, 65, 79–80, 86–7, 96

Blaker, Richard, writer, 30
Bourne, John, historian, 10, 94–5
Boyd, William, author, 77
Bracco, Rosa M., historian, 28, 34–5
Brest-Litovsk, Treaty of (1918), 9
British Expeditionary Force (BEF), 5, 7, 97–9
British Instructional Films, 38
British Official War Films, 13–14
Brogan, Hugh, historian, 77
Brooke, Rupert, poet, 28
Browne, Maurice, theatre producer, 34–5
Buchan, John, politician and author, 41–2

Cambrai, Battle of, 21, 98
Campaign for Nuclear Disarmament (CND),
   51
Carrington, Charles, historian, 32
casualties, 24–5, 44, 79, 100
Cave, Nigel, historian, 89, 92
Cecil, Hugh, historian, 30
Chapman, Guy, historian, 31–2
Charmley, John, historian, 100
Chilton, Charles, pioneer in the use of popular
   music in drama and documentaries, 63
Churchill, Winston, statesman and historian,
   42–5, and 49 (*The World Crisis*), 56
Clark, Alan, politician and historian, 60–1,
   64–5, 85, 100

conscription, 7, 51–2, 96 (in Canada)
Cruttwell, C. R. F. M., historian, 42
Cuban missile crisis 1962, 51

Dalton, Hugh, politician, 22
Danchev, Alex, historian, 59, 73
Dardanelles (and Gallipoli) operations, 24,
    43–4, 55, 58, 60; portrayed in *All the King's
    Men*, 78
Day-Lewis, Sean, author, 79
De Groot, Gerard, historian, 79
Dench (Dame) Judi, actress, 81
Dill, John, regimental officer in the First
    World War, general in the Second, 19
Doyle, Sir Arthur Conan, author, 41
Duff Cooper, Alfred, politician and author, 47

'Easterners and Westerners', 57
Eden, Anthony, statesman, 32
Edmonds, Charles, pen-name of Charles
    Carrington q.v., 32
Eksteins, Modris, historian, 36–7, 40
Essex, Tony, television producer, 68–9
Etaples, mutiny at, 14–15
Ewart, Wilfred, author, 30

Falls, Cyril, historian, 27, 30, 33
Farrar-Hockley, General Sir Anthony,
    historian, 64
Faulks, Sebastian, novelist, 76
Ferguson, Niall, historian, 100
Fletcher, Raymond, politician and contributor
    to *Oh What a Lovely War*, 59, 64
Foch, Ferdinand, marshal of France, 44, 91
Frankau, Gilbert, novelist, 30
Frankland, Noble, historian, 68–9
Freikorps, active in Baltic states, 24
French, David, historian, 92
French, Field Marshal Sir John, 62, 67
Fuller, Major-General J. F. C., 45
Fuller, John, historian, 94
Fussell, Paul, writer on war literature and
    culture, 12, 72, 76, 100

Gardner, Brian, historian, 63
Garnier, Edward, politician, 83
General Headquarters (GHQ) in France, and
    the press, 11, 18–19, 41; accused of living in
    luxury at Montreuil, 85–6
George. V, King, 60

Giles, John, founder of the Western Front
    Association q.v., 91
Grant, U. S., US general and president, 71
Graves, Robert, poet and author, 16, 30–1,
    33–4
Great War (The), television series, 68–70
Grey, Sir Edward, statesman, 4
Griffith, Paddy, historian, 92, 99
Grigg, John, politician and historian, 56–7
Gurner, Ronald, novelist, 30
Gwynn, Major-General Sir Charles, 48

Haig, David, writer, 77
Haig, Field Marshal Sir Douglas, 18, 22,
    42–7, 54, 58–72, 95–8, 101; his reputation
    debated on television, 78–80, 94
Haking, General Sir Richard, 95
Hastings, Max, journalist and historian, 85
Hattersley, Roy, politician, 80
Hiley, Nicholas, media historian, 12–13
Hindenburg, General Paul von, 8–9
Hindenburg Line, 20–1, 101
Hitler, Adolf, 56, 89
Holmes, Richard, historian, 90–1
Horne, Alistair, historian, 72
Howard, Sir Michael, historian, 60, 71
Hughes-Wilson, John, historian, 84
Hunter-Weston, General Sir Aylmer, 95
Hussey, John, historian, 79, 101
Hynes Samuel, writer on war literature and
    culture, author of *A War Imagined*, 38–40,
    48–9

Imperial War Museum, 55, 68, 78, 88, 93
Ireland, 5, 24
Ivanov, Eugene, Soviet naval attaché, 52

Japan, 3, 7
Jason, David, actor, 78
Jeffries, Stuart, journalist, 79
Jerrold, Douglas, author, 33, 39–40
Johnson, Lyndon B., US president, 53
Journey's End, play, 33–5, film, 38–9
Jünger, Ernst, soldier and author, 30–1

Keegan, Sir John, historian, 19–20, 96
Keeler, Christine, 52
Kelly, Sir David, diplomat, 32, –3
Kennedy, Paul, historian, 2–3, 6–7
King's College, London, 53–4

Kipling, Lt John (son of Rudyard), 77
Kitchener, Field Marshal Lord, 7, 12

Lady Chatterley's Lover, 52
Laffin, John, historian, 76, 78–9
Laird, Fiona, theatre director, 78
Larkin, Philip, poet, 52
Lawrence, Col. T. E., 46, 58
Lee, John, historian, 92
Liddell Hart, Sir Basil, historian, influential
    after 1918, 42, 45–6; and after 1945, 58–62,
    66, 71, 95; adviser for *The Great War*
    television series and *Purnell's* part-work
    history, 69–70
Liddell Hart Lecture (1997), 20–1
Liddle, Peter, historian, and the Liddle
    Collection, 93
Littlewood, Joan, theatre artist, 60, 63–5
Lloyd George, David, statesman, 4–5, 9, 22,
    44, 58, 62, 66, 71–2, 79; his *War Memoirs*,
    46–9
London School of Economics (LSE), 53
Loos, Battle of, 8, 19, 60, 77
Ludendorff, General Erich, 8, 20–1
Lusitania, 10

Mackinlay, Andrew, politician, 82–3
Malcolm, Derek, film critic, 67
Manning, Frederic, author, 29–30
March Retreat (1918) or German Spring
    Offensive, 14, 58, 80
Marne, Battle of the, 58
Marwick, Arthur, historian, 52–3
Massie, Allan, author, 85
Maurice, Major-General Sir Frederick, 48
Maxse, General Sir Ivor, 17
Middlebrook, Martin, historian, 63, 93–4
Milestone, Lewis, American film producer,
    37
Mills, Sir John, actor, 67
Milner, Lord, statesman, 42
Moltke, Field Marshal Helmuth von, 'the
    Elder', 71
Mons, Battle of, 38
Montague, C. E., journalist and author, 10, 29
Montgomery, Bernard, regimental officer in
    the First World War and senior commander
    in the Second, 19, 59
Moorehead, Alan, historian, 55
Morrell, Lady Ottoline, 16

national service (in Britain), 51–2
Nazi Germany, 56–7, 89
Northcliffe, Lord (Alfred Harmsworth),
    politician and newspaper proprietor, 18

Oh What a Lovely War, play, 59–60, 63–5, 73,
    96 and revival, 77–8; film, 66–8, 71, 73
Onions, Oliver, writer, 31
Owen, Wilfred, poet, 28, 31, 77–8, 81, 85, 88

Paget, Derek, historian, 66
Palestine, 46
Paris, Michael, historian, 38–9
Passchendaele, Battle of (including Third
    Ypres), 14, 18, 45–6, 72–3
Pitt, Barrie, historian, 70
Plumer, General Sir Herbert, 91, 95
Pollard, Alfred O., VC, war hero and author,
    30
Press Bureau (British), 12–13
Prior, Robin, historian, 97–100
Profumo, John, politician, 52
Prussian general staff (and militarism), 3, 9
Public Records Act (1967), 52
Purnell's History of the First World War, 70–1

Rawlinson, General Sir Henry, 17
Raymond, Ernest, novelist, 28–9
Read, Herbert, author, poet, publisher, 31
Reid, John, politician, 82–3
Remarque, Erich Maria, author, 35–8, 40
Rice Davies, Mandy, 52
Rivers, W. H., psychologist at Craiglockhart
    Hospital, 76–7
Robertson, Field Marshal Sir William, 44–5,
    62
Romania, 8
Rothermere, Lord (Harold Harmsworth),
    politician and newspaper proprietor, 18
Royal British Legion, 54, 82, 89
Russell, Bertrand, philosopher and author,
    16
Russia, 3, 8

Sassoon, Siegfried, poet and author, 31, 81,
    88; his anti-war protest, 15–17
Sheffield, Gary, historian, 22, 79, 86–7, 92,
    94, 96, 98
Sherriff, R. C., dramatist, 33–5, 38–9, 87
Simkins, Peter, historian, 92–3, 96

Simpson, Keith, politician and historian, 79, 83
Somerville, Christopher, author, 88
Somme, Battle of the, 8, 14, 18, 38, 45, 58, 62–3, 69, 76–8, 91, 94
Spanish influenza, 23–4
Staff College, Camberley, 18
Stevenson, David, historian, 9
Strachan, Hew, historian, 92
Strategic bombing, 57
Suez crisis (1956), 54

Taylor, A. J. P., historian, 1, 56, 61–3, 71–2
Teaching History, 88–9
Terraine, John, historian, 59, 68–9, 71–3, 90–1
Thiepval, war memorial at, 25
Thorpe, Adam, author, 78
Travers, Tim, historian, 97–8
Tuchman, Barbara, historian, 65

Unconditional Surrender (allied policy 1943–5), 57
United States of America, 6, 9, 64, 80
Unknown Warrior, 25

Verdun, Battle of, 8, 44, 63, 69, 91
Versailles, Treaty of (1919), 2
Vietnam War, 53–4

Ward, Stephen, osteopath, 52
Wark, Kirsty, television journalist, 79
Wells, H. G., author, 16
Western Front Association 87, 90
Wheen, A. W., translator of *All Quiet on the Western Front*, 35
Wilhelm II, Kaiser, 56
Wilson, A. N., author, 85
Wilson, Trevor, historian, 33, 79, 97–8, 100
Wilson, Woodrow, US president, 9, 64
Winter, Denis, historian, 76
Winter, Jay, historian, 24; joint producer of television series with Blaine Baggett, 80–2; founder of the *historial* at Péronne, 93
Wolfenden Committee, 52
Wolff, Leon, author, 59–60, 65

Ypres, Third Battle of (and see 'Passchendaele'), 38, 44, 59–62, 76, 79, 91
Ypres, Menin Gate war memorial, 25
Ypres, Museum of the First World War, 84
Young, Brigadier Peter, historian, 70